Mary Jones

Cambridge IGCSE®

Combined and Co-ordinated Sciences

Biology Workbook

CAMBRIDGE
UNIVERSITY PRESS

CAMBRIDGE
UNIVERSITY PRESS

University Printing House, Cambridge CB2 8BS, United Kingdom

One Liberty Plaza, 20th Floor, New York, NY 10006, USA

477 Williamstown Road, Port Melbourne, VIC 3207, Australia

314–321, 3rd Floor, Plot 3, Splendor Forum, Jasola District Centre,
New Delhi – 110025, India

103 Penang Road, #05-06/07, Visioncrest Commercial, Singapore 238467

Cambridge University Press is part of the University of Cambridge.

It furthers the University's mission by disseminating knowledge in the pursuit of
education, learning and research at the highest international levels of excellence.

www.cambridge.org
Information on this title: www.cambridge.org/9781316631041

© Cambridge University Press 2017

First published 2017

20 19 18 17 16 15 14 13 12 11 10 9

Printed in Great Britain by Ashford Colour Press Ltd.

A catalogue record for this publication is available from the British Library

ISBN 978-1-316-63104-1 Paperback

Contents

iii

Introduction

This workbook covers two syllabuses: Cambridge IGCSE Combined Science (0653) and Cambridge IGCSE Co-ordinated Sciences (0654). Before you start using this workbook, check with your teacher which syllabus you are studying and which papers you will take. You will sit either the Core paper or the Extended paper for your syllabus. If you are sitting the Extended paper, you will study the Core material and the Supplement material for your syllabus.

Once you know which paper you will be sitting, you can use the exercises in this workbook to help develop the skills you need and prepare for your examination.

The examination tests three different Assessment Objectives, or AOs for short. These are:

AO1 Knowledge with understanding

AO2 Handling information and problem solving

AO3 Experimental skills and investigations.

In the examination, about 50% of the marks are for AO1, 30% for AO2 and 20% for AO3. Just learning your work and remembering it is therefore not enough to make sure that you get the best possible grade in the exam. Half of all the marks are for AO2 and AO3. You need to be able to use what you've learned in unfamiliar contexts (AO2) and to demonstrate your experimental skills (AO3).

There are lots of activities in your coursebook which will help you to develop your experimental skills by doing practical work. This workbook contains exercises to help you to develop AO2 and AO3 further. There are some questions that just involve remembering things you have been taught (AO1), but most of the questions require you to use what you've learned to work out, for example, what a set of data means, or to suggest how an experiment might be improved.

These exercises are not intended to be exactly like the questions you will get on your exam papers. This is because they are meant to help you to develop your skills, rather than testing you on them.

There's an introduction at the start of each exercise that tells you the purpose of it – which skills you will be working with as you answer the questions.

For some parts of the exercises, there are self-assessment checklists. You can try using these to mark your own work. This will help you to remember the important points to think about. Your teacher should also mark the work and will discuss with you whether your own assessments are right.

There are sidebars in the margins of the book to show which material relates to each syllabus and paper. If there is no sidebar, it means that everyone will study this material.

Use this table to ensure that you study the right material for your syllabus and paper:

Cambridge IGCSE Combined Science (0653)		Cambridge IGCSE Co-ordinated Sciences (0654)	
Core	**Supplement**	**Core**	**Supplement**
You will study the material:	*You will study the material:*	*You will study the material:*	*You will study* **everything**. *This includes the material:*
Without a sidebar	Without a sidebar	Without a sidebar	Without a sidebar
	With a double grey sidebar	With a single grey sidebar	With a single grey sidebar
	With a double black sidebar	With a double grey sidebar	With a double grey sidebar
			With a single black sidebar
			With a double black sidebar

We would like to thank Cambridge International Examinations for permission to reproduce exam questions.

Chapter B1
Cells

Exercise B1.01   Observing and drawing organisms

This exercise will help you to improve your observation and drawing skills (AO3.3). You will also practise calculating magnification.

You need:

- specimens of two different fish
- a sharp HB (medium hard) pencil and a good eraser
- a ruler to measure in mm.

a   Observe the fish carefully. Look for similarities and differences between them.

b   On the blank page following, make a large drawing of one of the fish. You can turn the page sideways if this works better. Leave space around the drawing for labels.

c   Label your drawing to point out any interesting features of the fish.

Use the checklist below to give yourself a mark for your drawing. For each point, award yourself:
- **2 marks if you did it really well**
- **1 mark if you made a good attempt at it and partly succeeded**
- **0 marks if you did not try to do it, or did not succeed.**

Self-assessment checklist for drawing:

Check point	Marks awarded	
	You	Your teacher
You used a sharp pencil and rubbed out mistakes really thoroughly.		
You have drawn single lines, not many tries at the same line.		
You have drawn the specimen the right shape, and with different parts in the correct proportions.		
You have made a really large drawing, using the space provided.		
You have included all the different structures that are visible on the specimen.		
You have drawn label lines with a ruler, touching the structure being labelled.		
You have written the labels horizontally and neatly, well away from the diagram itself.		
Take 1 mark off if you used any shading or colours.		
Total (out of 14)		

12–14 Excellent.

10–11 Good.

7–9 A good start, but you need to improve quite a bit.

5–6 Poor. Try this same drawing again, using a new sheet of paper.

1–4 Very poor. Read through all the criteria again, and then try the same drawing.

d i Measure the actual length of the fish, in mm.

length of real fish = ... mm

ii Measure the same length on your drawing.

length on drawing = ... mm

iii Use your measurements to calculate the magnification of your drawing. Write down the equation you will use, and show your working.

magnification = ...

e Complete Table 1.01 to describe at least three differences between the two fish.

Feature	Fish 1	Fish 2

Table 1.01

Exercise B1.02 Animal and plant cells

> This exercise will help you to improve your knowledge of the structure of animal and plant cells, and give you more practice in calculating magnification.

The diagram shows an animal cell, and the outline of a plant cell. They are not drawn to the same scale.

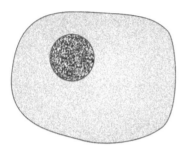   

a On the animal cell, label the following parts:

    cell membrane   **cytoplasm**   **nucleus**

b Complete the diagram of the plant cell, and then label the following parts:

    cell membrane   **cytoplasm**   **large vacuole containing cell sap**   **nucleus**
    chloroplast   **cell wall**   **membrane around vacuole**

c The actual maximum width of the animal cell is 0.1 mm.

    i   Measure the maximum width of the diagram of the animal cell, in mm ....

    ii   Calculate the magnification of the animal cell diagram. Show your working.

    magnification = ...

d The magnification of the plant cell diagram is × 80. Calculate the real height of the plant cell. Show your working.

    height = ...

Exercise B1.03 Drawing cells and calculating magnification

> This exercise helps you to improve your observation and drawing skills (AO3.3), as well as giving you more practice in calculating magnification.

Look carefully at Image B1.01 in the Cambridge IGCSE Combined and Co-ordinated Sciences Coursebook.

a **i** In the space below, make a large diagram of the largest cell (the one on the right of the photograph). You cannot see all of the cell, as its ends are out of the picture. Draw only the part that you can see.

ii Label these structures on your diagram. You will have to make a sensible guess as to which structure is the nucleus.

cell wall   **position of cell membrane**   **chloroplast**   **nucleus**

Use the checklist below to give yourself a mark for your drawing. For each point, award yourself:

- **2 marks if you did it really well**
- **1 mark if you made a good attempt at it and partly succeeded**
- **0 marks if you did not try to do it, or did not succeed.**

Self-assessment checklist for drawing:

Check point	Marks awarded	
	You	Your teacher
You used a sharp pencil and rubbed out mistakes really thoroughly.		
You have drawn single lines, not many tries at the same line.		
You have drawn the specimen the right shape, and with different parts in the correct proportions.		
You have made a really large drawing, using the space provided.		
You have included all the different structures that are visible on the specimen.		
You have drawn label lines with a ruler, touching the structure being labelled.		
You have written the labels horizontally and neatly, well away from the diagram itself.		
Take 1 mark off if you used any shading or colours.		
Total (out of 14)		

12–14 Excellent.

10–11 Good.

7–9 A good start, but you need to improve quite a bit.

5–6 Poor. Try this same drawing again, using a new sheet of paper.

1–4 Very poor. Read through all the criteria again, and then try the same drawing.

b The magnification of the photograph in Figure B1.6 is × 2000.

    i Calculate the real width of the largest cell in the photograph.
       Show your working.

width ....

ii Calculate the magnification of your drawing of the plant cell.

magnification = ...

Exercise B1.04 Organelles

This exercise tests your knowledge of the functions of organelles in animal and plant cells.

This list contains organelles that are found in cells.

cell membrane	cell wall	cytoplasm	chloroplast
mitochondrion	nucleus	ribosome	vacuole

Write the name of the organelle beneath its function.

a Contains chromosomes made of DNA, and controls the activity of the cell.

....

b An extra, strong layer surrounding a plant cell, made of cellulose.

....

c A jelly-like substance where many metabolic reactions happen.

....

d Every cell is surrounded by one of these. It controls what enters and leaves the cell.

....

e Some plant cells have these, but animal cells never do. This is where photosynthesis takes place.

....

f This is a space inside a cell that contains a liquid, for example cell sap.

....

Chapter B2
Movement in and out of cells

Exercise B2.01 Diffusion experiment

This exercise asks you to handle and interpret data collected during an experiment, and also to think about how the experiment was planned (AO3.4 and AO3.2).

A student did an experiment to test this hypothesis:

The higher the temperature, the faster diffusion takes place.

She took four Petri dishes containing agar jelly. She cut four holes in the jelly in each dish. She placed 0.5 cm³ of a solution containing a red pigment (coloured substance) into each hole. The following diagram shows the experimental set-up.

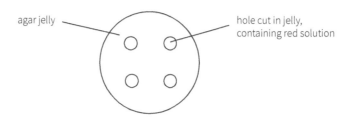

The student then covered the dishes and very carefully placed them in different temperatures. She left them for two hours. Then she measured how far the red colour had diffused into the agar around each hole. Table 2.01 shows the student's results.

Dish	Temperature / °C	Distance red colour had diffused into the jelly / mm				
		Hole 1	Hole 2	Hole 3	Hole 4	Mean (average)
A	10	2	3	2	3	
B	20	5	5	6	4	
C	40	9	11	8	10	
D	80	19	21	18	123	

Table 2.01

a Complete Table 2.01 by calculating the mean distances diffused by the red colour in each dish. (Give each distance to the nearest whole number, because this is how the student's measurements were taken.) Write your answers in the table.

9

b Do the results support the student's hypothesis? Explain your answer.

....

....

....

....

c State **four** variables that the student kept constant in her experiment, or that she should have kept constant.

1 ....

2 ....

3 ....

4 ....

d Explain why it was a good idea to have four holes in each dish, rather than just one.

....

....

10

e Suggest **two** significant sources of experimental error in this investigation.

1 ....

2 ....

Exercise B2.02   How plants take up water

> This exercise checks that you haven't forgotten about cell structure. It also develops your ability to use your knowledge in a new situation (AO2).

Plants take up water into their roots, from the soil. They have tiny hairs on their roots which help with this. The hairs are called root hairs, and each one is part of a single cell. The diagram shows a root hair cell.

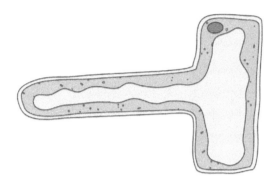

a   State **two** structural features of this cell that are typical of plant cells but not animal cells.

1   ....

2   ....

b   On the diagram of the cell, label a partially permeable membrane. Use a ruler to draw the labelling line.

c   The concentration of the cytoplasm and the cell sap inside the root hair cell is greater than the concentration of the water in the soil around the root hair cell. Use your knowledge of osmosis to explain how water is absorbed into the root hair cell.

....

....

....

....

....

d   Root hair cells are tiny, and there are hundreds of them on each plant root. Suggest how this helps to increase the rate at which the plant can take up water.

....

....

Exercise B2.03 Osmosis and potatoes

> In this exercise, you will practise drawing a results chart and recording numerical results in it (AO3.3). You will also construct a graph and evaluate the results (AO3.4). Question d is a good test of your understanding of osmosis, and your ability to use your knowledge in a new situation (AO2).

A student investigated the effect of different concentrations of sugar solutions on some potato cylinders. He took a large potato and used a cork borer to cut out several cylinders, each exactly the same diameter. He trimmed the peel off the ends of the cylinders, and then cut them into exactly 1 cm lengths. He then measured the mass of each piece.

He placed one piece of potato in each of six beakers. He then covered each piece with either water, or one of five different concentrations of sugar solution. He used the same volume of solution in each beaker. The student left the potato pieces in the beakers for 30 minutes. Then he removed them from the beakers, blotted them dry with filter paper and measured their mass again. His results are shown in Table 2.02.

Before	piece A = 5.2 g	piece B = 5.1 g	piece C = 4.9 g
	piece D = 5.0 g	piece E = 5.1 g	piece F = 5.2 g
Solutions	A, distilled water	B, 0.1% sugar solution	C, 0.2% solution
	D, 0.5% solution	E, 0.8% solution	F, 1.0% solution
After	A = 5.5 g	B = 5.2 g	C = 4.9 g
	D = 5.3 g	E = 5.0 g	F = 5.0 g

Table 2.02

a In the space below, draw your own results table and fill in the student's results. Include a row or column showing the change in mass. Take care to head each column and row fully, with units.

b Decide if there are any anomalous results. If you think there are, draw a ring around them.

c Display the results as a line graph on the grid below. Put concentration of solution on the *x*-axis and change in mass on the *y*-axis. Remember to include units in your axis labels.

d Use your knowledge of osmosis to explain the results.

....

....

....

....

....

....

....

....

e Suggest how the student could have changed his method to make his results more reliable.

....

....

....

f The student's teacher suggested that it would have been better if he had calculated the percentage change in mass of each piece of potato, rather than just the change in mass. Do you agree? Explain your answer.

....

....

....

....

Use the checklist below to give yourself a mark for your results chart. For each point, award yourself:
- **2 marks if you did it really well**
- **1 mark if you made a good attempt at it and partly succeeded**
- **0 marks if you did not try to do it, or did not succeed.**

Self-assessment checklist for results charts:

Check point	Marks awarded	
	You	Your teacher
You have drawn the chart with a ruler.		
Headings have correct units in each column and row (there are no units inside the cells of the table).		
Your chart is easy for someone else to read and understand.		
If your chart contains readings, all are to the same number of decimal places (for example, 15.5, 9.0).		
Total (out of 8)		

8	Excellent.
7	Good.
5–6	A good start, but you need to improve quite a bit.
3–4	Poor. Try this same results chart again, using a new sheet of paper.
1–2	Very poor. Read through all the criteria again, and then try the same results chart again.

Use the checklist below to give yourself a mark for your graph. For each point, award yourself:

- **2 marks if you did it really well**
- **1 mark if you made a good attempt at it and partly succeeded**
- **0 marks if you did not try to do it, or did not succeed.**

Self-assessment checklist for graphs:

Check point	Marks awarded	
	You	Your teacher
You have drawn the axes with a ruler, and used most of the width and height of the graph paper for the axis labels.		
You have used a good scale for the x-axis and the y-axis, going up in 1s, 2s, 5s or 10s.		
You have included the correct units with the scales on both axes.		
You have plotted each point precisely and correctly.		
You have used a small, neat cross for each point.		
You have drawn a single, clear line – either by ruling a line between each pair of points or by drawing a well-positioned best-fit line.		
You have ignored any anomalous results when drawing the line.		
Total (out of 14)		

12–14 Excellent.

10–11 Good.

7–9 A good start, but you need to improve quite a bit.

5–6 Poor. Try this same graph again, using a new sheet of paper.

1–4 Very poor. Read through all the criteria again, and then try the same graph again.

15

Chapter B3
Biological molecules

Exercise B3.01 Carbohydrates

> This exercise will give you practice in constructing results charts (AO3.3) and drawing conclusions (AO3.4), as well as helping you to remember important facts about carbohydrates.

A student carried out tests on two foods. This is what she wrote in her notebook.

Starch test – food A went brown, food B went black

Benedict's reagent – food A went orange-red, food B went blue

a   Construct a results table and complete it to show the student's results. Think carefully about the best way of showing what she did, what she was testing for, what results she obtained and what these results mean.

b   Complete Table 3.01 about carbohydrates.

Type of carbohydrate	Example	Role in living organisms
sugar	glucose	
		the form in which carbohydrates are transported in plants
polysaccharide		the form in which plants store energy
	glycogen	

Table 3.01

Exercise B3.02 Testing a hypothesis

> This exercise will help you to remember the biuret test for proteins. It will also help you to improve your skills in planning experiments (AO3.2). Your teacher may allow you to carry out your experiment – if so, you are almost certain to find you want to make some changes to it. That is good – it is what most scientists do.

The biuret test is used to test foods for proteins. The intensity of the colour obtained depends on the concentration of protein in the sample being tested.

Plan an investigation to test this hypothesis:

Milk from cows contains a higher concentration of protein than milk from goats.

a First, describe how you would do the biuret test.

....

....

....

b Now think about how you could use this test to test the hypothesis.

i What variable would you change in your experiment?

....

....

ii What would you keep the same? Try to think of at least three variables you would keep the same.

....

....

....

iii What would you measure in your experiment?

....

iv How would you measure it?

....

....

v If the hypothesis is correct, what results would you expect to obtain?

....

....

Exercise B3.03 Writing enzyme questions

> This exercise will make you think hard about some of the facts you know about enzymes, which should help you to remember them.

Write a multiple-choice question for each of the following sets of answers. Then underline the correct answer to your question.

1 ....

....

....

A amylase   **B** catalase   **C** lipase   **D** protease

2 ....

....

....

A denatured   **B** killed   **C** slowed down   **D** speeded up

3 ....

....

....

A fat   **B** protein   **C** maltose   **D** starch

Now write two more multiple-choice questions about enzymes. For each question, indicate the correct answer by underlining it.

4 ....

....

....

5 ....

....

....

....

18

Exercise B3.04 Lipase experiment

> This exercise will help you improve your ability to analyse and evaluate data (AO3.4), and to plan experiments (AO3.2). It will also reinforce your knowledge of the role of lipase.

An experiment was carried out to investigate the effect of temperature on the enzyme lipase. Lipase digests fats to fatty acids (which have a low pH) and glycerol.

A solution of lipase was made and equal volumes of it were added to five test tubes. The tubes were treated as follows:

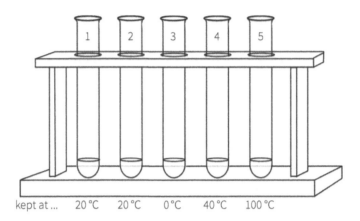

kept at ...   20 °C   20 °C   0 °C   40 °C   100 °C

All five tubes were kept at these temperatures for five minutes.

A pH meter was used to measure the pH of the liquid in each tube.

Equal volumes of milk (which contains fat) were then added to tubes 2, 3, 4 and 5.

Every two minutes, the pH of the contents of each tube was tested as before. The results are shown Table 3.02.

Tube	1	2	3	4	5
Temp / °C	20				
Milk added?		yes			
pH at: 0 min	7.0	7.0	7.0	7.0	7.0
2 min	7.0	6.8	7.0	6.7	7.0
4 min	7.0	6.7	7.0	6.5	7.0
6 min	7.0	6.6	7.0	6.3	7.0
8 min	7.0	6.6	6.9	6.2	7.0
10 min	7.0	6.5	6.9	6.2	7.0

Table 3.02

a What is the substrate of the enzyme lipase?

....

b What are the products when lipase acts on its substrate?

....

c   Explain why the pH becomes lower when lipase acts on its substrate.

....

....

d   Complete Table 3.02 by filling in all the blank cells.

e   Explain why the pH did not change in tube 1.

....

f   Explain why the pH did not change in tube 5.

....

g   Explain why the results for tubes 2 and 3 differed from each other.

....

....

....

....

h   The student who did this experiment concluded that the optimum temperature for lipase is 40 °C.
    What are your opinions about this conclusion?

....

....

....

i   Suggest some changes that could be made to this experiment to obtain a more reliable or more precise value
    for the optimum temperature of lipase.

....

....

....

j Explain how you could use lipase to investigate whether cow's milk contains a higher concentration of fat than goat's milk. (Remember to think about the variables you will need to control.)

....

....

....

....

....

....

....

....

....

....

....

....

....

....

....

....

....

....

Exercise B3.05 Finding the optimum pH for amylase

> **This exercise leads you through designing an experiment (AO3.2), and thinking about variables you will change, variables you will control and variables you will measure. Your teacher may let you do your experiment when you have designed it, in which case you can come back to your original design and make changes to it that you think might have worked better.**

The pH of a liquid can be kept steady by adding a buffer solution to it. You can obtain buffer solutions for any pH value you require. You can use a pH meter to measure the pH.

Plan an investigation to test this hypothesis:

The optimum pH for amylase is 7.5.

Here is some of the apparatus you might like to include.

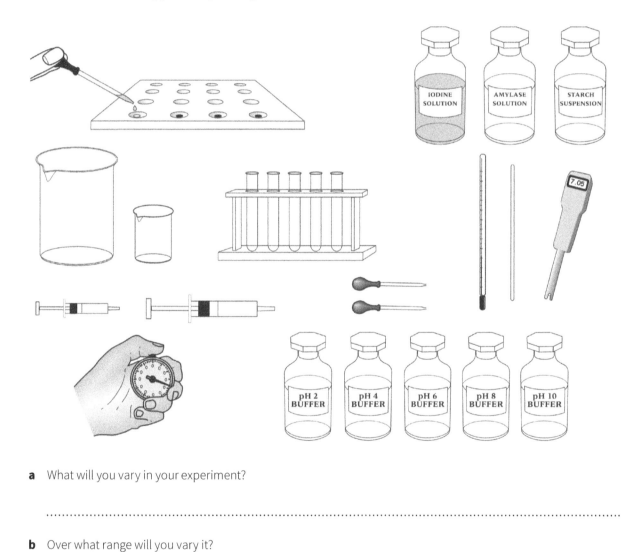

a What will you vary in your experiment?

....

b Over what range will you vary it?

....

c How will you vary it?

....

....

d What variables will you keep constant in your experiment? How will you do this?

....

....

....

e What results will you measure in your experiment, how will you measure them and when will you measure them?

....

....

....

....

f Briefly outline the steps you will follow in your investigation.

....

....

....

....

....

....

....

....

....

....

....

....

g Draw a results table in which you could record your results.

h Sketch a graph to show the results you would expect if the hypothesis is correct.

Use the checklist below to give yourself a mark for planning your experiment. For each point, award yourself:

- **2 marks if you did it really well**
- **1 mark if you made a good attempt at it and partly succeeded**
- **0 marks if you did not try to do it, or did not succeed.**

Self-assessment checklist for planning an experiment:

Check point	Marks awarded	
	You	Your teacher
You have stated the variable to be changed (independent variable), the range of this variable and how you will vary it.		
You have stated at least three important variables to be kept constant (and not included ones that are not important).		
You have stated the variable to be measured (dependent variable), how you will measure it and when you will measure it.		
You have drawn up a results chart into which you can write your results.		
If a hypothesis is being tested, you have predicted what the results will be if the hypothesis is correct.		
Total (out of 10)		

10	Excellent.
8–9	Good.
5–7	A good start, but you need to improve quite a bit.
3–4	Poor. Try this same plan again, using a new sheet of paper.
1–2	Very poor. Read through all the criteria again, and then try the same plan again.

Exercise B3.06 How enzymes work

You will need to think about how an enzyme interacts with its substrate in order to answer these questions. It is important to use correct scientific terminology when you are answering part c.

The diagram shows an enzyme and a molecule of its substrate, maltose. The enzyme is able to split a maltose molecule into two glucose molecules.

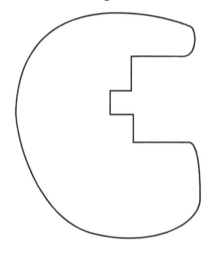

a   On the diagram, label the active site of the enzyme.

b   In the space below, draw two new diagrams to show:

   i   the enzyme and substrate bound together

   ii   the enzyme and products after the reaction is completed.

c Use the diagrams to explain each of the following statements.

    i An enzyme is specific for one type of substrate.

    ....

    ....

    ....

    ii Enzyme-catalysed reactions happen faster at 20 °C than at 10 °C.

    ....

    ....

    ....

    ....

    iii Enzyme-catalysed reactions happen faster at 30 °C than at 50 °C.

    ....

    ....

    ....

    ....

Chapter B4
Plant nutrition

🔑 **KEY TERMS**

photosynthesis: the process by which plants manufacture carbohydrates from raw materials using energy from light

Exercise B4.01   How a palisade cell obtains its requirements

> Writing these descriptions will help you to summarise and remember how a palisade cell obtains the things it needs for photosynthesis, and the fate of the products.

Write short descriptions in each box in the following diagrams, to explain how a palisade cell in a leaf obtains its requirements for photosynthesis, and what happens to the products. Use each of these words at least once.

air space   diffusion   epidermis   osmosis   phloem   starch

root hair   stoma   transparent   sucrose   xylem

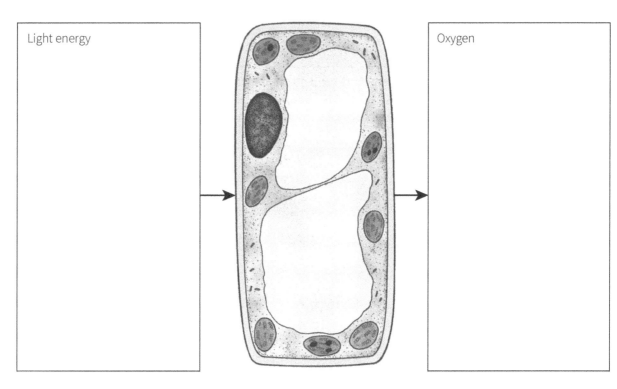

Light energy

Oxygen

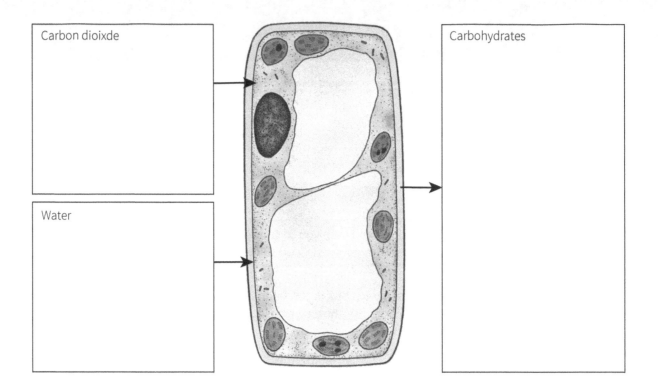

Carbon dioixde		Carbohydrates
Water		

Exercise B4.02 Sun and shade leaves

You don't need to know about sun and shade leaves, so don't worry – you don't have to learn facts about them. This exercise is about observing carefully and using what you can see, as well as what you already know about leaves, to work out (rather than just remember) answers to questions (AO2).

Some of the leaves on a tree spend most of the day in bright sunlight, while others are in the shade. The diagrams show sections through a leaf growing in the shade and a leaf growing in the sunlight.

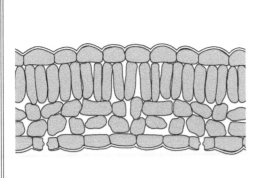

shade leaf

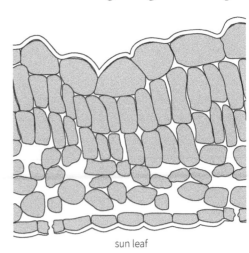

sun leaf

a Label these tissues on the shade leaf diagram:

upper epidermis   **palisade mesophyll**

spongy mesophyll   **lower epidermis**

b Put a few green spots in each cell that you would expect to contain chloroplasts on the shade leaf diagram.

c Complete Table 4.01 to compare the structures of each of these parts of the leaves.

Part of leaf	Sun leaf	Shade leaf
cuticle		
palisade mesophyll		
spongy mesophyll		

Table 4.01

d Suggest an explanation for the difference in the cuticle that you have described in Table 4.01.

....

....

e Suggest an explanation for the difference in the palisade layer that you have described in Table 4.01.

....

....

....

....

Exercise B4.03 Analysing data about rates of photosynthesis

In this exercise, you can practise drawing a line graph (AO2) and analysing data to draw conclusions and suggest explanations (AO2 and also AO3.4). It will also help you to check your understanding of limiting factors.

An experiment was performed to find out how fast a plant photosynthesised as the concentration of carbon dioxide in the air around it was varied. The results are shown in Table 4.02.

Percentage concentration of carbon dioxide	Rate of photosynthesis in arbitrary units	
	Low light intensity	High light intensity
0.00	0	0
0.02	20	33
0.04	29	53
0.06	35	68
0.08	39	79
0.10	42	86
0.12	45	89
0.14	46	90
0.16	46	90
0.18	46	90
0.20	46	90

Table 4.02

a Plot these results on the grid provided.

You can mark your graph using the self-assessment checklist for graphs.

Use the checklist below to give yourself a mark for your graph. For each point, award yourself:

- **2 marks if you did it really well**
- **1 mark if you made a good attempt at it and partly succeeded**
- **0 marks if you did not try to do it, or did not succeed.**

Self-assessment checklist for graphs:

Check point	Marks awarded	
	You	Your teacher
You have drawn the axes with a ruler, and used most of the width and height of the graph paper for the axis labels.		
You have used a good scale for the x-axis and the y-axis, going up in 1s, 2s, 5s or 10s.		
You have included the correct units with the scales on both axes.		
You have plotted each point precisely and correctly.		
You have used a small, neat cross for each point.		
You have drawn a single, clear line – either by ruling a line between each pair of points or by drawing a well-positioned best-fit line.		
You have ignored any anomalous results when drawing the line.		
Total (out of 14)		

12–14 Excellent.

10–11 Good.

7–9 A good start, but you need to improve quite a bit.

5–6 Poor. Try this same graph again using a new sheet of paper.

1–4 Very poor. Read through all the criteria again and then try the same graph again.

b State the carbon dioxide concentration of normal air.

....

c Use your graph to find the rate of photosynthesis in normal air in high light intensity.

....

d Up to what concentration is carbon dioxide a limiting factor for photosynthesis in low light intensity?

....

e Above this concentration (your answer to **d**), what is the limiting factor for photosynthesis?

....

f Farmers and market gardeners often add carbon dioxide to the air in glasshouses where crops are growing. Use your graph to explain the advantage of doing this.

....

....

....

....

g It is expensive to add carbon dioxide to glasshouses. Suggest a suitable concentration of carbon dioxide to add to a glasshouse in high light intensity, to obtain a good financial return from the sale of the crop. Explain your answer.

....

....

....

....

Chapter B5
Animal nutrition

Exercise B5.01 Diet

> This exercise helps you to practise using information to work out the answers to questions (AO2).

Table 5.01 shows the energy and nutrients contained in 100 g of five foods.

Food	Energy / kJ	Protein / g	Fat / g	Carbohydrate / g	Calcium / mg	Iron / mg	Vitamin C / mg	Vitamin D / mg
apple	150	0.2	0	9.0	0	0.2	2	0
chicken, roast	630	25.0	5.0	0	0	0.8	0	0
egg, scrambled	1050	10.0	23.0	0	60	2.0	0	1.8
rice, boiled	500	2.0	0.3	30.0	0	0	0	0
spinach, boiled	130	5.0	0.5	1.5	600	4.0	25	0

Table 5.01

a What pattern can you see in the kinds of food that contain carbohydrate?

....

b Scrambled egg has the highest energy content per gram of all of the foods in the table. What data in the table could explain why the energy content of scrambled egg is so high?

....

....

c Use the data in the table to work out which of the five foods contains the greatest mass of water per 100 g. Show your working.

....

d A person is suffering from anaemia. Which foods from the table would be most helpful for her to include in her diet? Explain your answer.

....

....

....

....

Exercise B5.02 Functions of the digestive system

This exercise will help you to remember the roles of the different parts of the digestive system. The diagram is not the same as the one in your coursebook, Figure B5.08 – you need to be prepared to interpret different versions of diagrams.

The diagram shows a number of boxes which contain descriptions of things that happen to food as it moves along the alimentary canal. Draw label lines to the appropriate parts of the digestive system on the diagram.

Saliva is secreted into here from the salivary glands.

Gastric juice is made here, containing pepsin and hydrochloric acid.

Pancreatic juice flows into here.

Amylase breaks down starch to maltose.

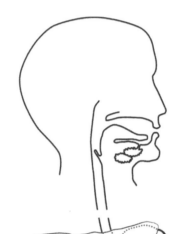

Mastication increases the surface area of food.

Amylase breaks down starch to maltose.

Bile salts emulsify fats.

Pepsin breaks down proteins to polypeptides.

Sodium hydrogencarbonate neutralises acid from the stomach.

Lipase breaks down fats to fatty acids and glycerol.

Exercise B5.03 Tooth decay data analysis

> These questions help you to develop your abilities to find and describe patterns in data and suggest explanations for them (AO2).

A study was carried out into the effect of two factors on the number of decayed teeth in five-year-old children in three towns. The two factors were:

- whether or not fluoride was added to the drinking water, or if the water naturally contained fluoride (fluoride is known to strengthen tooth enamel)

- the general standard of living of the family, measured using a score from –30 (very high living standards) to +50 (very low living standards).

The results are shown in the graph.

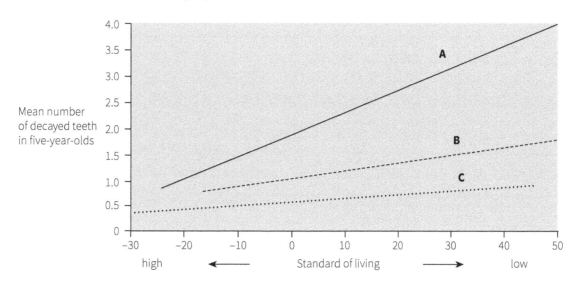

A town where the water does not naturally contain fluoride, and where fluoride was not added

B town where water does not naturally contain fluoride, and where fluoride was added

C town where water naturally contains fluoride

a Describe the effect of standard of living on tooth decay in town A.

....

....

....

b Suggest reasons why a low standard of living may have the effect you describe in your answer to part **a**.

....

....

....

c Describe the effect of adding fluoride to drinking water that does not naturally contain fluoride.

....

....

....

d Suggest reasons for the differences in the results for town B and town C.

....

....

....

....

Exercise B5.04 Vitamin D absorption

> This exercise asks you to describe data provided in a graph, in words. It's a good idea to focus on parts of the graph where the line changes gradient or direction, and to quote some coordinates from the graph, remembering to give the units of the figures that you refer to.

In an investigation into the absorption of vitamin D from the alimentary canal, a volunteer ate a measured quantity of vitamin D on a piece of toast. Blood samples were then taken from her at intervals over a period of 72 hours, and the amount of vitamin D in each blood sample was measured. The results are shown in the graph.

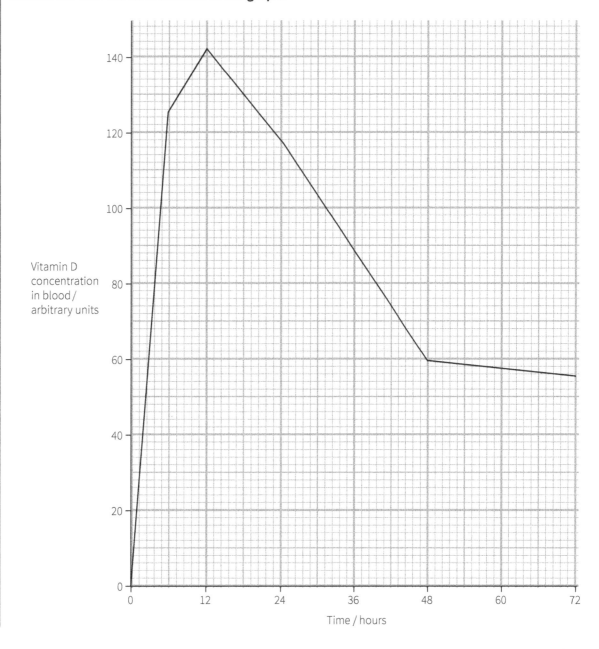

a Describe the changes in the amount of vitamin D in the blood over the 72-hour period.

....

....

....

....

....

b Name the part of the alimentary canal in which vitamin D is absorbed into the blood.

....

c List **three** other substances that are absorbed in this part of the alimentary canal.

....

d Describe how this part of the alimentary canal is adapted to make absorption efficient.

....

....

....

....

....

e Explain why vitamin D does not need to be digested before it is absorbed.

....

....

f The volunteer was asked not to expose her skin to sunlight during the investigation. Suggest why this was done.

....

....

....

Chapter B6
Transport in plants

KEY TERMS

transpiration: loss of water vapour from plant leaves by evaporation of water at the surfaces of the mesophyll cells followed by diffusion of water vapour through the stomata

Exercise B6.01 A transpiration experiment

This exercise gives you practice in recording results (AO3.3), constructing graphs (AO3.4), drawing conclusions and evaluating the reliability of results (also AO3.4).

A student investigated this hypothesis:

Transpiration happens more quickly in windy conditions than in still air.

The diagram shows the apparatus that the student used.

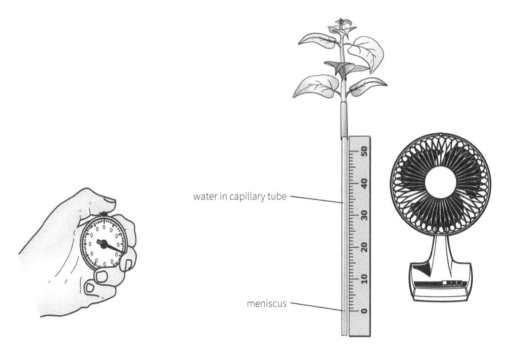

water in capillary tube

meniscus

The student placed a leafy shoot in the apparatus and stood it in a quiet place in the lab, where the air was still. He read off the position of the meniscus every two minutes for ten minutes.

He then placed the fan close to the apparatus and switched it on. He continued to read the position of the meniscus every two minutes for the next ten minutes. These are the results he wrote down.

start 0 cm	2 min, 2.8	4 min, 6.1	6 min, 10.0
8 min, 12.9	10 min, 16.2	12 min, 21.8	14 min, 27.9
16 min, 31.1	18 min, 39.5	20 min, 44.9	

a Draw a suitable results chart, and fill it in.

b Plot these results on the grid provided. Draw a vertical line upwards from the *x*-axis, to divide the graph into the period of time when the air was still, and when it was moving. Draw two best-fit lines, one on either side of this dividing line. If you think any of the results are anomalous, then ignore them when drawing your best-fit lines.

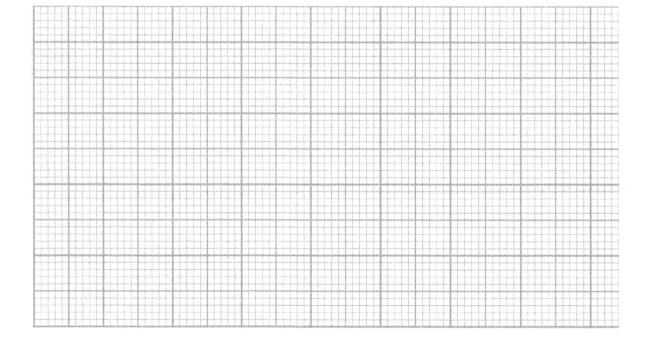

c Use the graph to calculate the mean rate of movement, in cm per minute, of the meniscus in still air and in moving air.

still air ....   moving air ....

d Do the results support the student's hypothesis? Explain your answer.

....

....

....

e Suggest any significant sources of error in this experiment. (For example, did the student control all the important variables? Did his method really measure what he thought he was measuring?)

....

....

....

....

....

....

Chapter B7
Transport in mammals

Exercise B7.01 Double and single circulatory systems

> Constructing a diagram in a slightly different way is often a good way of checking that you really do understand a concept. You will also need to use your knowledge to explain how and why one type of circulatory system might have advantages over another (AO2).

The diagram shows a simple plan of a double circulatory system.

a   In the space above, draw a similar diagram to show a single circulatory system.

b   Name **one** organism that has a double circulatory system.

   ....

c   Name **one** organism that has a single circulatory system.

   ....

d   Many animals with double circulatory systems have higher metabolic rates than those with single circulatory systems.

   Suggest an explanation for this relationship.

   ....

   ....

   ....

   ....

   ....

Exercise B7.02 The heart in a fetus

> This exercise will make you think hard about the double circulatory system of a human and how it works, and use your previous knowledge to work out some likely explanations (AO2).

The diagram shows the heart of a fetus (a baby developing in its mother's uterus).

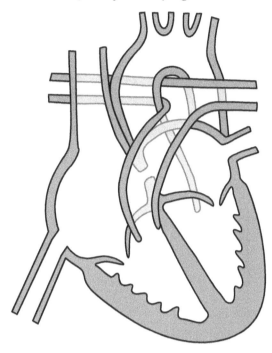

In a fetus, the lungs do not work. The fetus gets its oxygen from the mother, to whom it is connected by the umbilical cord. This cord contains a vein, which carries the oxygenated blood to the fetus's vena cava.

a   On the diagram, write the letter **O** in the chamber of the heart that first receives oxygenated blood in an **adult person**.

b   On the diagram, write the letters **OF** in the chamber of the heart that first receives oxygenated blood in a **fetus**.

c   If you look carefully at the diagram, you can see that there is a hole in the septum between the left and right atria. Suggest the function of this hole in the heart of a fetus.

   ....

   ....

   ....

d   When the baby is born, it takes its first breath. The hole in the septum of the heart quickly closes. Explain why this is important.

   ....

   ....

   ....

Exercise B7.03 Risk of heart attack

In this exercise, you will practise picking out relevant information from a table of data and using it to suggest answers to questions about a real-life situation (AO2).

Table 7.01 shows part of a chart that doctors use to predict the likelihood of someone having a heart attack. Diabetes is an illness caused by a faulty mechanism for regulating the concentration of glucose in the blood. It can be controlled, but not cured.

| | Percentage of women who are expected to have a heart attack within five years | | | | | | | |
| | Age 40 | | Age 50 | | Age 60 | | Age 70 | |
	No diabetes	With diabetes	No diabetes	With diabetes	No diabetes	With diabetes	No diabetes	With diabetes
Non-smokers	1	3	3	7	5	12	7	23
Smokers	4	7	6	13	12	22	15	33

Table 7.01

a   Imagine that you are a doctor. A woman patient is 54 years old. She has diabetes and she smokes. What will you tell her about her chance of having a heart attack within the next five years?

   ....

   ....

b   What will you tell her she should do to reduce her chances of having a heart attack? How will you use the chart to explain this to her?

   ....

   ....

   ....

   ....

c   Suggest how the figures used in this chart have been determined.

   ....

   ....

   ....

Exercise B7.04 Changes in the blood system at high altitude

This exercise will give you further practice in describing patterns in bar charts. You will also use what you know about the functions of the blood to suggest explanations for a set of data, and to make predictions (AO2).

The air is much thinner at high altitude, so less oxygen is drawn into the lungs with each breath. When a person who normally lives at low altitude travels into high mountains, changes occur in their blood system.

The bar charts shows changes in the pulse rate and the number of red blood cells in a person who moved to high altitude, stayed there for two years, and then returned to sea level.

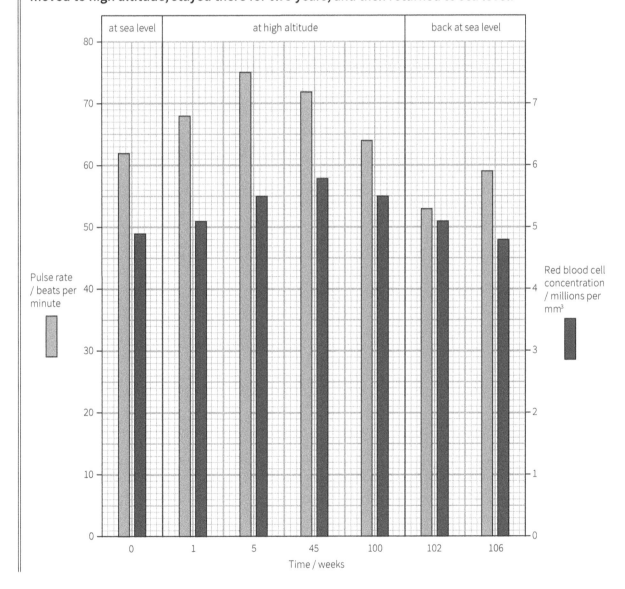

a Describe the changes in the pulse rate over the period shown in the bar chart.

....

....

....

....

....

b Describe the changes in the number of red blood cells over the period shown in the bar chart.

....

....

....

....

....

c State the function of red blood cells.

....

d Suggest a reason for the change in the number of red blood cells during the first year of the study.

....

....

....

....

e Muscles need a good supply of oxygen in order to be able to work hard and fast. Athletes often train at high altitude for several months before a major competition that will be held at a lower altitude. Use the data in the bar chart to suggest how this might help them to perform well in the competition.

....

....

....

....

....

Chapter B8
Respiration and gas exchange

KEY TERMS

aerobic respiration: the chemical reactions in cells that use oxygen to break down nutrient molecules to release energy

anaerobic respiration: the chemical reactions in cells that break down nutrient molecules to release energy, without using oxygen

Exercise B8.01 Effect of temperature on the rate of respiration

This is a planning exercise (AO3.2). It has not been broken up into sections, because by now you are probably getting the hang of planning good experiments and should be able to organise your answer yourself. Your teacher may allow you to carry out your experiment once your design has been checked.

Plan an investigation to test this hypothesis:

Germinating peas respire faster as temperature increases, up to an optimum.

Think carefully about controlling variables, what you will measure and when, and how you will record and interpret your results. Predict what the results will be if the hypothesis is correct.

....

....

....

....

....

....

....

....

....

....

....

....

....

Exercise B8.02   Effect of animals and plants on the carbon dioxide concentration in water

> This exercise will make you think about photosynthesis and respiration, as well as interpreting results and making predictions (AO2).

A student had a fish tank, in which she kept tropical fish. She knew it was meant to be a good idea to keep living plants in the tank as well. She wanted to find out how the plants affected the concentration of carbon dioxide in the water.

The diagram shows the apparatus that she set up. She used hydrogencarbonate indicator solution because it is yellow when it contains a large amount of carbon dioxide, orange with a small amount and red when it contains no carbon dioxide at all.

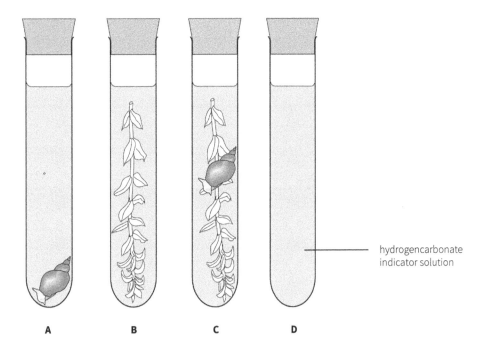

The student left all four tubes in a sunny place for 30 minutes. When she looked at the tubes again, she found the indicator had turned yellow in tube **A**, deep red in tube **B**, and stayed orange in tubes **C** and **D**.

a   Draw a results chart and fill it in to show the student's results.

b Explain the results in each tube. (Remember that living organisms all respire all the time, and that plants also photosynthesise in the light.)

Tube A ....

....

Tube B ....

....

Tube C ....

....

Tube D ....

....

c Predict the results that would be obtained if all the tubes were left in the dark.

....

....

d Discuss what these results and your predictions in **c** suggest about whether or not it is good to have living plants in a fish tank.

....

....

....

....

Exercise B8.03 Gas exchange surfaces in rats

There is further practice in plotting line graphs here, as well as interpreting data and thinking about their possible implications (AO2). When making comparisons of data, try to link your statements with words such as 'however', or 'but'. As always, make sure that you quote some actual figures in your comparisons. Better still, you could make a comparative calculation, such as the total change in the ratios for males and for females, or the difference between males and females at a particular age.

Rat lungs have a similar structure to human lungs. Researchers measured the surface area of the alveoli in the lungs of female and male rats of different ages. They also measured the mass of each rat, and calculated the number of square centimetres of alveolar surface area per gram of body mass.

Their results are shown in Table 8.01.

Age / days	Ratio of alveolar surface area to body mass / cm² per gram	
	Females	Males
21	21.6	23.1
33	15.4	15.2
45	12.9	12.1
60	13.4	10.9
95	13.4	9.4

Table 8.01

a   Plot line graphs to display these data. Plot both curves on the same pair of axes. (Take care with the scale for the x-axis.)

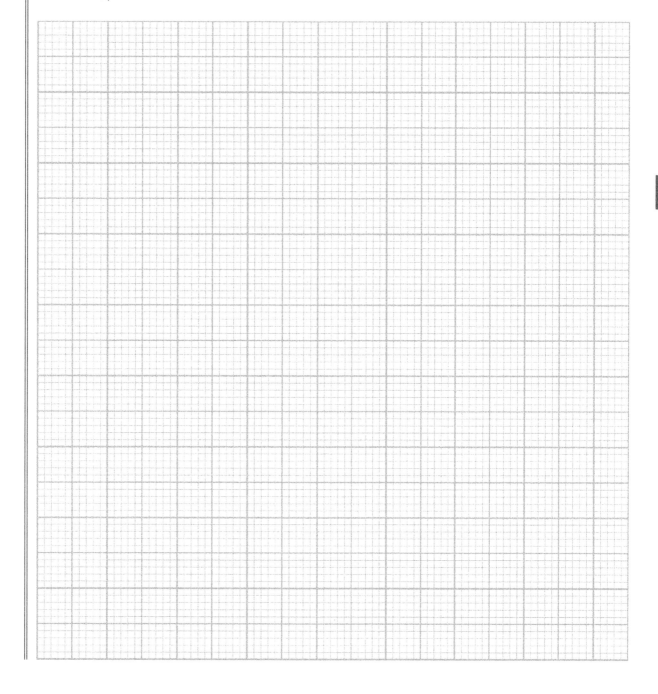

b Suggest why the researchers recorded the ratio of alveolar surface area to body mass, rather than just the alveolar surface area.

....

....

....

c Compare the results for female and male rats.

....

....

....

....

....

....

d Female rats are able to become pregnant when they are about 60 days old. Their lungs then have to supply oxygen for themselves, and also for their developing offspring.

Suggest how the data in Table 8.01 could relate to this fact.

....

....

....

....

....

Chapter B9
Co-ordination and homeostasis

Exercise B9.01 Caffeine and reaction time

> You should be getting quite confident at planning experiments by now, so there are no reminders here about all the different things you need to include (AO3.2). You'll find it quite tricky to control variables in this one. You may be able to try out your experiment when you've planned it.

Reaction time is the time between receiving a stimulus and responding to it.

Plan an experiment to test this hypothesis:

Consuming drinks containing caffeine decreases reaction time.

Exercise B9.02 Accommodation in the eye

Doing this exercise – preferably without looking anything up – will be a good test of how well you understand how the eye changes in order to focus on objects at different distances, which is called accommodation. Use a ruler to draw the light rays on your diagram, and take great care to show clearly where they change direction and where they are brought to a focus.

The diagram shows an eye focused on a distant object.

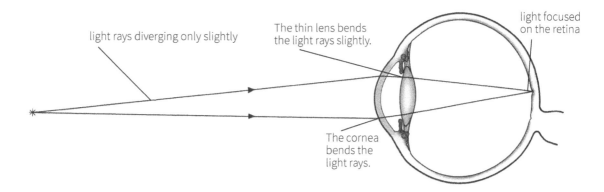

light rays diverging only slightly

The thin lens bends the light rays slightly.

light focused on the retina

The cornea bends the light rays.

a Complete the diagram below to show the eye when it is focused on a nearby object. Add labels to match those on the first diagram.

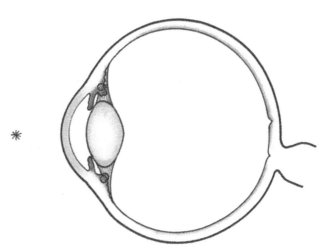

b Describe how the changes that you have shown are brought about. Use these words in your description:

ciliary muscles   **lens**   **suspensory ligaments**

....

....

....

....

....

c Accommodation in the eye is a reflex action.

    i Explain what is meant by a reflex action.

    ....

    ....

    ii Suggest what could be the stimulus that brings about this reflex action.

    ....

    ....

d As people get older, their lenses become less able to change shape. Suggest how this may affect their vision.

....

....

....

Exercise B9.03 Auxin and tropism

> For the line graphs in this exercise, you are asked to draw best-fit lines. Your lines should be smooth, and should have roughly the same number of points above them as below them. Start both lines exactly at 0,0, but they do not necessarily have to go exactly through the final point.

A plant growing in a pot was placed on its side, in conditions of uniform light. The diagram shows the appearance of the plant after three days.

a This response is known as negative gravitropism. Explain what is meant by the term negative gravitropism.

....

....

b A scientist measured the concentration of auxin in the upper and lower surfaces of the plant shoot. She also measured the percentage increase in length of the upper and lower surface of the plant shoot over a period of one hour.

Tables 9.01 and 9.02 show her results.

Time / minutes	Percentage increase in length	
	Upper surface	Lower surface
10	0.9	1.1
20	1.1	2.2
30	1.6	3.8
40	2.0	5.3
50	2.3	6.6
60	2.8	7.6

	Upper surface	Lower surface
Concentration of auxin / arbitrary units	1.0	1.4

Table 9.01

Table 9.02

i On the grid provided, draw line graphs to show the results in Table 9.02. Draw both lines on the same set of axes. Draw best-fit lines for each set of results.

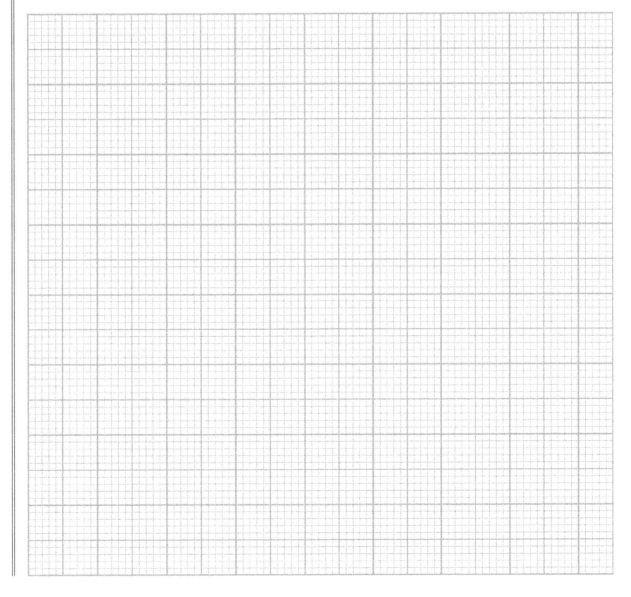

ii Use the results in Tables 9.01 and 9.02 to explain what made the plant shoot grow upwards after the pot was turned onto its side.

....

....

....

....

....

Exercise B9.04 Endotherms and ectotherms

> In this exercise, you are asked to use your knowledge of temperature regulation in humans, and some new data, to work out answers to questions (AO2).

Humans are endotherms – we are able to regulate our body temperatures, keeping the core body temperature roughly constant no matter what the temperature of our environment. Many animals, however, are ectotherms. Their core temperature varies according to the temperature of their environment.

The graph shows the core temperatures of six animals in different environmental temperatures.

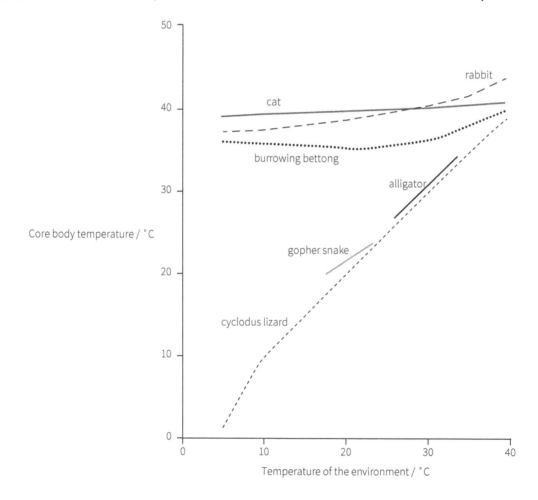

a Write the name of each animal in the correct column of Table 9.03.

Endothermic animals	Ectothermic animals

Table 9.03

b Cyclodus lizards, gopher snakes and alligators need to eat much less food than cats, rabbits or bettongs. Use the information in the graph above to explain why.

....

....

....

....

c Use the graph above to compare the probable activity of a cat and a cyclodus lizard when the environmental temperature is 5 °C.

....

....

....

d Cats are predators. Rabbits are herbivores, preyed on by cats and other mammals. Explain the advantages to cats and rabbits of being endothermic.

....

....

....

....

....

Exercise B9.05 Diabetes

> **This exercise is about interpreting data shown in a graph, and relating this to your knowledge of the regulation of blood glucose (AO2).**

In some people, the control of blood glucose concentration does not work correctly.

In type I diabetes, the pancreas does not secrete insulin when it should.

a In what circumstances does the pancreas normally secrete insulin?

....

The graph shows the concentration of glucose in the blood of two people, after they had eaten a meal containing starch at time 0. One person had type I diabetes, and the other did not.

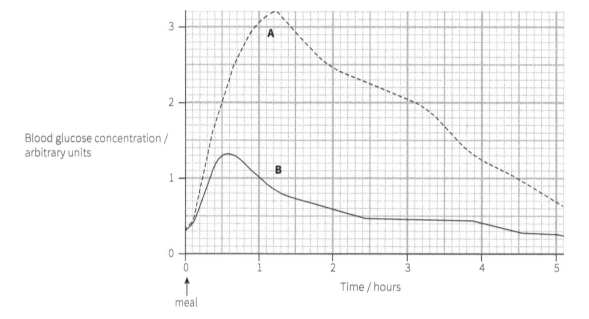

b Explain why the concentration of glucose in the blood increases when a person has eaten a meal containing starch.

....

....

....

....

....

c   Suggest which person, A or B, has type I diabetes. Explain your answer fully.

....

....

....

....

....

....

....

d   Explain why it is important to keep the concentration of glucose in the blood neither too high nor too low.

....

....

....

....

....

....

....

asexual reproduction: a process resulting in the production of genetically identical offspring from one parent

sexual reproduction: a process involving the fusion of the nuclei of two gametes (sex cells) to form a zygote and the production of offspring that are genetically different from each other

pollination: the transfer of pollen grains from the male part of the plant (anther of stamen) to the female part of the plant (stigma)

Exercise B10.01 Pollination in forests of different shapes and sizes

> This exercise presents the results of some research relating to deforestation. Although this is not covered until Chapter 14, you probably know a little about it already and will be able to make some sensible suggestions when answering questions (AO2). You will also need to draw conclusions (AO3.4) and think about planning a further investigation (AO3.2).

All over the world, forests are being cut down and destroyed. Small patches are often left behind, and research is being carried out to see how the shape and size of these patches affects the animals and plants that live in them. One piece of research looked at the pollination of holly flowers by butterflies in three different areas of forest. The areas were:

A: a set of patches of forest all connected to each other by long, narrow tree-covered areas ('corridors')

B: a set of patches of forest the same size as those in A, but not connected

C: a set of smaller patches of forest, not connected.

The butterflies that pollinated the holly flowers were known to spend most of their time at the edges of forests, rarely penetrating into deep forest for very long.

The researchers inspected samples of holly flowers in each forest area, and counted the numbers of ovaries that were turning into fruits. They then calculated the mean number of fruits per flower in each area. The bar chart shows their results.

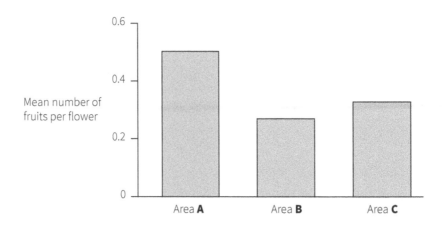

a Describe the results shown in the bar chart.

....

....

....

b Using the information in the introduction to this exercise, suggest explanations for the results obtained.

....

....

....

....

c It is likely that your suggested reasons are not actually proved by these results. Suggest how the researchers could modify their original experiment to test one of your suggestions more fully and reliably.

....

....

....

....

....

d It could be argued that this research suggests it is better to leave small patches of forest rather than large ones. However, most conservationists would say that this is not correct. With reference to this research, and using your own thoughts about the importance of forests, discuss these two points of view.

....

....

....

....

....

....

....

....

Exercise B11.01 Gametes

> Answer this question without looking anything up – you should be able to do it from memory. Remember to draw label lines with a ruler, and make sure that the end of the line touches the part of the cell that you are labelling. The labels should be written horizontally and should not overlap the diagram.

The diagrams show human female and male gametes.

a Use black or dark blue to label all the structures on each gamete that you would find in any animal cell.

b Use red or another contrasting colour to label all the structures on each gamete that are adaptations for their specialised functions. Explain how each feature that you label helps the cell to perform its function.

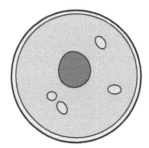

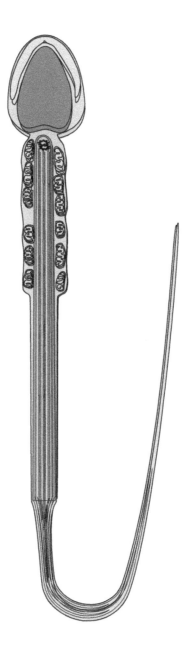

Exercise B11.02 Gas exchange in the placenta and lungs

This exercise asks you to use data to make a comparison between two very different body organs – the placenta and the lungs – which have some functions in common (AO2). It would be a good idea to plan your answers to parts bii and c before you begin to write.

The placenta is an organ that allows a mother's blood and her fetus's blood to be brought very close together, without mixing. Substances are exchanged by diffusion between the two blood systems.

The lungs also contain surfaces where substances are exchanged by diffusion. (This is not the case in the fetus, whose lungs do not function until after it is born.)

Table 11.01 shows some features of the placenta and the lungs in a human.

Feature	Placenta	Lungs
Total surface area / m²	16	55
Thickness of the barrier across which substances must diffuse / µm	3.5	0.5
Approximate rate of blood flow / cm³ per minute	500	5000

Table 11.01

a Explain how the structure of the lungs provides the large surface area shown in the table.

....

....

....

b Oxygen moves by diffusion across the exchange surface in both the placenta and the lungs.

i State precisely where oxygen moves to and from in the lungs.

....

....

ii Explain fully why the net movement of oxygen is in this direction.

....

....

....

....

c   Use the data in the table, and your knowledge of the features of gas exchange surfaces, to explain why more oxygen can be absorbed per minute across the lungs than across the placenta.

....

....

....

....

....

....

....

....

Chapter B12
Inheritance

KEY TERMS

inheritance: the transmission of genetic information from generation to generation

chromosome: a thread-like structure of DNA, carrying genetic information in the form of genes

gene: a length of DNA that codes for a protein

allele: any one of two or more alternative forms of a gene

haploid nucleus: a nucleus containing a single set of unpaired chromosomes, e.g. in gametes

diploid nucleus: a nucleus containing two sets of chromosomes, e.g. in body cells

mitosis: nuclear division giving rise to genetically identical cells

meiosis: reduction division in which the chromosome number is halved from diploid to haploid, resulting in genetically different cells

genotype: genetic make-up of an organism in terms of the alleles present

phenotype: the observable features of an organism

homozygous: having two identical alleles of a particular gene. Two identical homozygous individuals that breed together will be pure-breeding

heterozygous: having two different alleles of a particular gene, not pure-breeding

dominant: an allele that is expressed if it is present

recessive: an allele that is only expressed when there is no dominant allele of the gene present

Exercise B12.01 Fruit fly inheritance

In this exercise, you will practise using a genetic diagram to predict the results of crosses between organisms.

Fruit flies, *Drosophila melanogaster*, are often used for research into genetics.
The diagram shows a fruit fly.

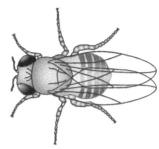

Fruit flies can have normal wings or vestigial (really small) wings. The allele for normal wings, **N**, is dominant. The allele for vestigial wings, **n**, is recessive.

a   Complete Table 12.01 to show the possible genotypes and phenotypes for fruit fly wings.

Genotype	Phenotype

Table 12.01

b Complete the genetic diagram to predict the genotypes and phenotypes of the offspring of a heterozygous normal-winged fly and a vestigial-winged fly.

phenotypes of parents   normal wings   vestigial wings

genotypes of parents   ....

gametes   ( ) and ( )   all ( )

gametes from
vestigial-winged fly

( )

gametes from
normal-winged fly

( )

( )

c The two flies had 82 offspring.

Predict approximately how many of these would have vestigial wings.

....

....

Exercise B12.02 Black and chestnut horses

This exercise is all about being able to use genetic terms correctly, and drawing correct genetic diagrams (AO1 and AO2). Remember that, when you show the gametes that can be produced by each parent, you only need to show *two* if there are *two different types* of gametes produced. If only one type of gamete is possible, then you need only show that one.

In horses, the colour of the coat is determined by genes. One gene determines whether or not the black pigment, melanin, is produced. Horses with the genotype **EE** or **Ee** are black, while horses with the genotype **ee** are chestnut (brown).

a Write down:

  i the symbol for the allele that allows melanin to be produced

  ....

  ii the genotype of a heterozygous horse

  ....

  iii the phenotype of a horse that is homozygous recessive.

  ....

b A black stallion was mated with a chestnut mare. The foal that was born was chestnut.

  i What was the genotype of the black stallion? Explain how you worked this out.

  ....

  ....

  ....

  ii Construct a genetic diagram, similar to the one in Exercise **B12.01**, to explain how the chestnut foal was produced.

iii If the same stallion and mare are bred together again, what are the chances of the second foal being chestnut? Explain your answer.

....

....

....

Exercise B12.03 Pedigree

This exercise asks you to work out genotypes, given some information about phenotypes in a family (AO2). You will also use your knowledge of genetics to think about the advice that a counsellor might give to a member of this family.

The family tree shows the incidence of a genetic disease called PKU in four generations of a family.

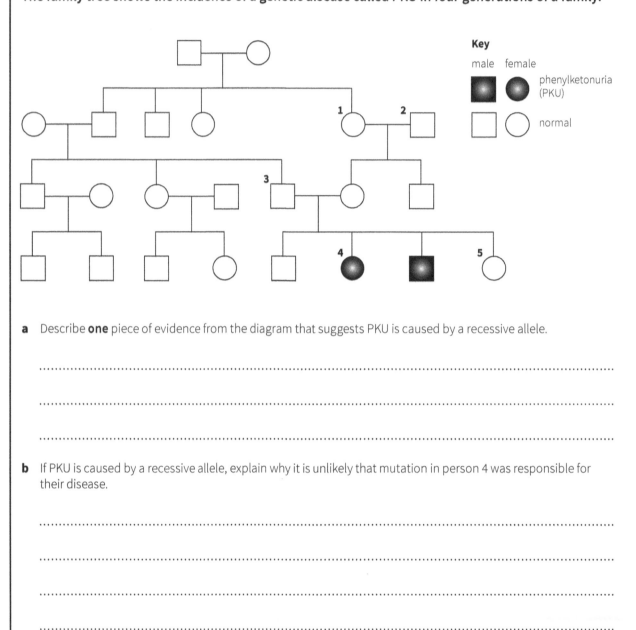

Key

male   female

■ ● phenylketonuria (PKU)

□ ○ normal

75

a Describe **one** piece of evidence from the diagram that suggests PKU is caused by a recessive allele.

....

....

....

b If PKU is caused by a recessive allele, explain why it is unlikely that mutation in person 4 was responsible for their disease.

....

....

....

....

c   Deduce the genotypes of persons 1, 2, 3 and 4. Use the symbol **q** for the PKU allele and the symbol **Q** for the normal allele.

....

....

....

....

....

d   Person 5 is worried that her children might have PKU. She talks to a genetic counsellor. What might she be told?

....

....

....

....

....

....

Chapter B13
Variation and inheritance

mutation: a change in a gene or chromosome

adaptation: the process, resulting from natural selection, by which populations become more suited to their environment over many generations

variation: differences between individuals of the same species

Exercise B13.01 Water hyacinth experiment

There is a tough magnification calculation in this exercise, using a unit you may not be familiar with. Don't worry – you are not supposed to know this unit – the task is about being able to use your understanding of magnification and the information given to work out the answer to a problem (AO2). (It's not easy, though!) The exercise will also help you to look carefully at data and make comparisons (also AO2), and to think about adaptations of plants that grow in water.

Water hyacinths are aquatic plants that originally came from Brazil but now grow in waterways in many tropical countries. They are sometimes used to help to clean up polluted water, as they are able to take up pollutants such as heavy metals.

An experiment carried out in China investigated differences in the structure of the leaf epidermis of water hyacinth plants grown in clean water and in polluted water.

The diagram and Table 13.01 show some of their results.

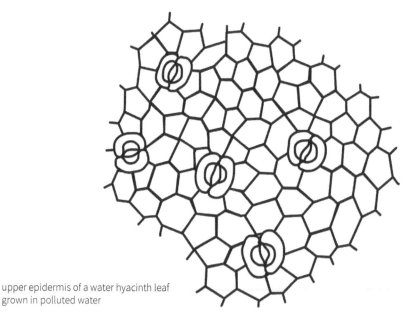

upper epidermis of a water hyacinth leaf grown in polluted water

Type of water	Upper or lower epidermis	Mean width of stomatal pore / μm	Mean length of guard cell / μm	Mean number of stomata per mm²
clean	upper	4	7	2.83
	lower	4	7	3.32
polluted	upper	3	5	2.80
	lower	3	5	2.83

Table 13.01

a   From the data in the table, what is the mean length of a guard cell in the upper epidermis of a water hyacinth leaf grown in polluted water?

....

b   Measure the length, in mm, of a guard cell in the diagram of the epidermis of a water hyacinth leaf.

.... mm

Now convert your answer in mm to an answer in μm. 1 mm = 1000 μm

.... μm.

Now use your answer to **a**, and your answer to **b** in μm above, to calculate the magnification of the diagram. Write down the formula that you use, and show your working.

....

c   Explain how the results in the table for water hyacinth leaves grown in clean water indicate that this plant is adapted for growing in water.

....

....

....

d Compare the characteristics of the leaf epidermis of the plants growing in clean water with plants growing in polluted water.

....

....

....

....

....

Exercise B13.02 Big-horn sheep

In this exercise, you will use your understanding of natural selection to try to work out what has caused a change in the characteristics of big-horn sheep (AO2).

Big-horn sheep live on rocky mountain sides in Canada. The males have very large horns. The size of their horns is caused by their genes.

a i Name the part of a cell that contains the genes.

....

ii In which cells in the big-horn sheep's body will the gene for horn size be present?

....

b Hunters kill big-horn sheep and keep their horns as trophies. They kill the sheep with the largest horns. The graph shows how the average size of the horns in a population of big-horn sheep changed between 1970 and 2005.

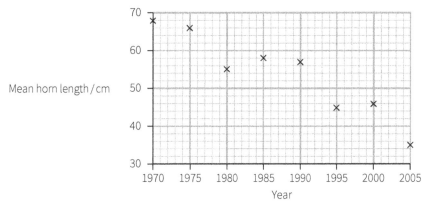

Mean horn length / cm

Explain how hunting of big-horn sheep could have caused the general trend shown in the graph.

....

....

....

....

c In summer it may be very hot in the mountains, but in winter it is very cold.

i Explain how the big-horn sheep's sweat glands can help to keep them cool in summer.

....

....

....

ii Explain how vasoconstriction can help to keep the sheep warm in winter.

....

....

....

[Cambridge IGCSE Co-ordinated Sciences 0654 Paper 3 Q4 b, c & d June 2006]

Exercise B13.03 Goats on an island

> This is another exercise that tests your understanding of several different parts of the syllabus, and asks you to use your knowledge and understanding to suggest explanations and make predictions (AO2). It's not actually a true story, but it could be!

In the nineteenth century, a ship travelling across the southern Pacific Ocean stopped at an island to collect fresh water. The sailors left one male goat, **P**, and two female goats, **Q** and **R**, on the island, hoping that they would breed and so provide food if the ship stopped there again.

a Goats **P**, **Q** and **R** all had short hair. They were all homozygous for allele **A**. However, a mutation happened in the testes of goat **P**, so that some of its sperm contained a new allele, **a**. Allele was recessive, and coded for long hair.

   i What is meant by the term 'mutation'?

     ....

     ....

   ii Explain why none of the offspring of goats **P**, **Q** and **R** had long hair.

     ....

     ....

     ....

   iii In the following year, some of the offspring from the three original goats bred with each other and with their parents. Some of their offspring did have long hair.

     Assuming that no new mutations appeared, explain how this happened. (You may use a genetic diagram if it makes your answer clearer.)

     ....

     ....

     ....

     ....

b The winters on the island were very cold. The goats needed to eat more food in winter to keep themselves warm. The long-haired goats did not need as much food as the short-haired goats.

    i Suggest why the long-haired goats did not need as much food as the short-haired goats during the winter.

....

....

....

....

    ii Twenty years after the goats were first introduced to the island, almost all of the goat population had long hair. Explain how this would have happened.

....

....

....

....

....

Adapted from [Cambridge IGCSE Co-ordinated Sciences 0654 Paper 3 Q6 b & c November 2003]

Exercise B13.04 Selective breeding for high milk yield

> This exercise contains some real data about the effects of artificial selection to try to develop herds of cows that produce more milk than usual. You will need to use your knowledge of selection pressures and their effects to make sense of the data and suggest explanations for the results (AO2). For the last part of the question, you'll need to think back to work you covered much earlier in your course.

Dairy cattle are kept to produce milk. The milk is produced and stored in the cow's udder. In 1965, a long experiment was begun to find out if artificial selection could increase the milk yield of cows. In one set of cows, artificial selection for high milk yield was carried out in each generation. These were called the **selected line**.

In the other set, there was no artificial selection. These were called the **control line**.

Both sets of cows were kept under the same conditions. The mean milk yield from the cows that were born in each year from 1965 to 1990 was calculated. The results are shown in the graph.

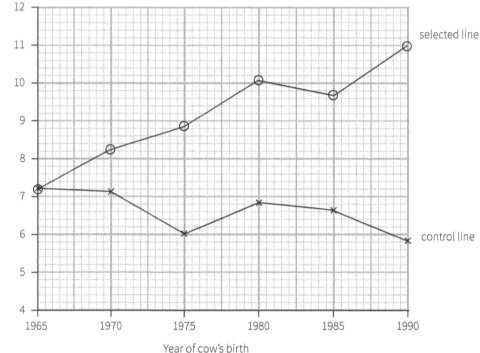

a Calculate the change in mean milk yield per cow between 1965 and 1990 for

  i   the selected line,

   ....

  ii the control line.

   ....

b Describe how artificial selection would have been carried out in the selected line.

....

....

....

....

c Suggest a reason for the results for the control line.

....

....

....

d The researchers also looked at the costs of health treatment in each of the two breeding lines. Table 13.02 shows some of the results.

Health problem	Cost of treatment in selected line / $	Cost of treatment in control line / $
mastitis (inflammation of the udder)	43	16
lameness	10	6

Table 13.02

84

i Suggest an explanation for the results shown in the table.

....

....

....

ii State and explain **one** reason, other than health treatment costs, why it would be more expensive to keep the cows from the **selected line** than the cows from the **control line**.

....

....

[Cambridge IGCSE Co-ordinated Sciences 0654 Paper 3 Q3 November 2007]

Chapter B14
Organisms and their environment

Exercise B14.01 Energy transfer in a food chain

This exercise involves a percentage calculation – remember to show your working clearly. You'll also need to think about how to explain quite difficult ideas clearly.

The diagram shows the quantity of energy contained within four trophic levels of a food chain.

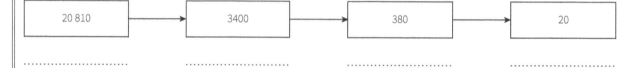

| 20 810 | 3400 | 380 | 20 |

a What is meant by the term 'trophic level'?

....

....

b Underneath each box in the diagram above, write the correct term for the organisms in that trophic level.

c i Calculate the percentage of energy in the first trophic level that is transferred to the fourth trophic level. Show your working.

    ii   Describe where all the rest of the energy goes.

....

....

....

d Use the information in the diagram to explain:

    i   why the populations of predators are normally smaller than the populations of their prey

....

....

....

....

    ii   why food chains rarely have more than four or five links.

....

....

....

Exercise B14.02 Eutrophication

> **You'll need to use your understanding of the effects of pollution by fertilisers on aquatic organisms to answer these questions (AO2). Some of the questions also require you to remember some facts covered much earlier in your biology course.**

A farmer sprayed fertilisers containing ammonium nitrate onto a field in which young wheat seedlings were growing.

a Explain why farmers often add nitrogen-containing fertilisers to the soil where crops are growing.

....

....

....

b Some of the fertiliser was washed into a river which ran alongside the wheat field.

The graph shows how this affected the numbers of bacteria, algae and fish in the river, downstream from the wheat field. It also shows how it affected the oxygen concentration.

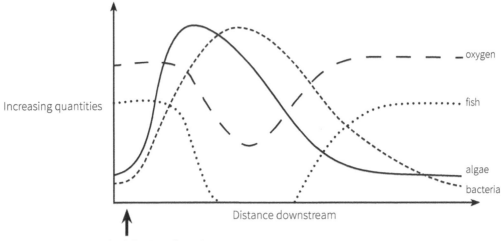

i Explain the shape of the curve for the numbers of algae.

....

....

....

ii With reference to the curves for bacteria and oxygen in the graph, explain the shape of the curve for fish.

....

....

....

....

[Cambridge IGCSE Co-ordinated Sciences 0654 Paper 3 Q7 a & c June 2003]

Exercise B14.03 Introduced species in New Zealand

> **This exercise is about one of the ways in which humans can cause harm to the environment.
> You are asked to look carefully at a set of data, and then to use this and your own knowledge to
> make predictions (AO2).**

New Zealand has been separated from the other land masses on Earth for millions of years. Fossils show that very few land-living mammals ever evolved there, but birds and bats were able to colonise. Until humans arrived, there were no predatory animals, and the native birds had not evolved adaptations that would help them to avoid predation.

Humans probably first arrived in New Zealand about 1500 years ago. Unintentionally, they brought rats with them, and since then have introduced other mammals. This has affected the native species.

a   Suggest why birds, and bats but not other mammals, were able to colonise New Zealand.

....

....

b   Use the theory of natural selection to suggest why many New Zealand birds are not able to fly. (This is quite a tricky question. You will need to think about selection pressures, and the costs to a bird of being able to fly.)

....

....

....

....

....

....

....

....

....

c Introduced animals can also harm populations of native plants. Nikau palms are found only in New Zealand and its surrounding islands, such as Great Barrier Island. Researchers counted the numbers of Nikau palm seedlings in areas where rats have been trapped and removed, and areas where no trapping was done. The results are shown in the bar chart.

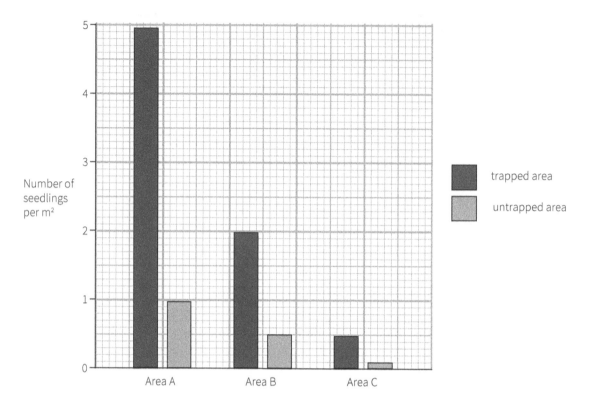

89

d Use the data in the bar chart to suggest how removing rats could affect the population of Nikau palms on Great Barrier Island.

....

....

....

....

Answers

Exercises include questions from past Cambridge exam papers and other questions written by the authors. Answers to all questions, including past paper questions, have been written by the authors.

Chapter B1 Cells

Exercise B1.01 Observing and drawing organisms

a, b, c Use the self-assessment checklist to assess the drawing and labelling.

d Check the measurements and calculation against the student's drawing.

e Look for clear, comparable points opposite each other.

Exercise B1.02 Animal and plant cells

a

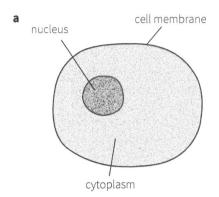

b

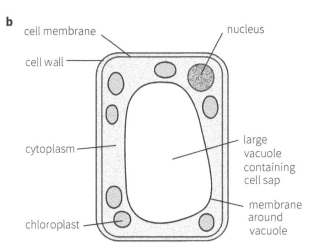

c Answer provided when we know the final size of the image

d Answer provided when we know the final size of the image

Exercise B1.03 Drawing cells and calculating magnification

a

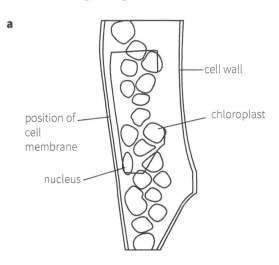

Use the self-assessment checklist to assess the drawing and labelling.

b i Answer provided when we know the final size of the image

ii Answer provided when we know the final size of the image

Exercise B1.04 Organelles

a nucleus

b cell wall

c cytoplasm

d cell membrane

e chloroplasts

f vacuole

Chapter B2 Movement in and out of cells

Exercise B2.01 Diffusion experiment

a See Table A2.01

Dish	Temperature / °C	Distance red colour diffused into jelly / mm				
		Hole 1	Hole 2	Hole 3	Hole 4	Mean (average)
A	10	2	3	2	3	3
B	20	5	5	6	4	5
C	40	9	11	8	10	10
D	80	19	21	18	23	20

Table A2.01

b Yes. As temperature increased, the distance the red colour diffused through the jelly increased. As the dishes were all left for the same period of time, this must mean the colour was moving faster in the warmer dishes. A doubling of the temperature caused the distance diffused by the colour to roughly double.

c The four most important variables to be controlled are: concentration of the solution of red pigment; size of hole in the jelly; depth of jelly in the dish; volume of solution placed in the hole.

d This allowed for a mean to be calculated. It improves the reliability of the results.

e Measurement of the distance diffused, because the 'edge' between the colour and the uncoloured jelly will not be very distinct. Some dye may have got into the jelly before the dishes are transferred to their final temperatures (especially as they were carried). Time taken for the dye and jelly in each dish to reach their final temperature – the dye won't have been at the correct temperature for the entire duration of the experiment.

Exercise B2.02 How plants take up water

a cell wall, large vacuole

b Label line to the cell surface membrane, or to the membrane around the vacuole.

c Water molecules move randomly. There is a greater concentration of them outside the cell than inside, so more will (by chance) move into the cell than out of it, through the partially permeable cell surface membrane. The solutes in the cell cannot get out through the partially permeable membrane. (Some students may answer in terms of water potential. The water potential of the solution outside the cell is higher than that inside, so water moves down its water potential gradient.)

d This provides a large surface area, so more water can pass across the surface at any one time.

Exercise B2.03 Osmosis and potatoes

a The table should have rows or columns for the percentage concentration of the solution, and rows or columns for the mass of potato pieces, with the unit g in the heading. Students should also calculate the change in mass. The following is an example of a suitable results table (see Table A2.02).

Percentage concentration of solution	Mass / g		
	Before soaking	After soaking	Change
0.0	5.2	5.5	+0.3
0.1	5.1	5.2	+0.1
0.2	4.9	4.9	0
0.5	5.0	5.3	+0.3
0.8	5.1	5.0	−0.1
1.0	5.2	5.0	−0.2

Table A2.02

b The mass of the potato piece soaking in 0.5% solution has increased, but it would be expected to decrease. This does not follow the pattern of the other results and so is anomalous.

91

c Look for the following features on the graph:
- 'Percentage concentration of solution' on the *x*-axis, and 'Change in mass / g' on the *y*-axis
- suitable scales
- all points plotted correctly (allow 0.5 mm tolerance) as crosses or as encircled dots
- either a best-fit line, drawn as a smooth curve with equal numbers of points above and below the line, or points joined with straight lines drawn with a ruler; the anomalous result should be ignored.

d The 0 and 0.1% solutions had a higher water potential than inside the potato cells, so water moved in by osmosis and made the cells increase in mass. The 0.2% solution had a water potential equal to that of the potato cells, so there was no net movement of water into or out of the cells (the same amount went in as came out) so there was no change in mass. The solutions with higher concentrations than this had water potentials lower than that of the potato cells, so water moved out of the cells by osmosis and their mass therefore decreased.

e Have several pieces of potato in each solution, and calculate a mean change in mass for each.

f Yes, this would have been better because the original masses of the potato pieces were not identical. Calculating percentage change would give a fairer comparison between the pieces – it would avoid discrepancies caused by this uncontrolled variable.

Chapter B3 Biological molecules

Exercise B3.01 Carbohydrates

a Look for a single ruled table (see Table A3.01) with fully headed rows and columns.

Food	Result of test with iodine	Result of test with Benedict's	Conclusion
A	brown	orange-red	contains reducing sugar but not starch
B	black	blue	contains starch but not reducing sugar

Table A3.01

Students might decide to have two separate columns for the conclusions, one for starch and one for reducing sugar, which would be fine.

b See Table A3.02

Type of carbohydrate	Example	Role in living organisms
sugar	glucose	provides energy; released by respiration; also the form in which carbohydrates are transported in mammalian blood
	sucrose	the form in which carbohydrates are transported in plants
polysaccharide	starch	the form in which plants store energy
	glycogen	the form in which animals store energy

Table A3.02

Exercise B3.02 Testing a hypothesis

a Add dilute sodium hydroxide (or potassium hydroxide) and very dilute copper sulfate solution to the milk. A purple colour indicates the presence of protein. (Alternatively, biuret reagent could be added.)

b **i** The variable to be changed is the type of milk – cow's milk and goat's milk.

ii The most important variables to be controlled are: the volume of milk, the age of the milk, the temperature of the milk, the volume and concentration of reagents added to it, the time left before the intensity of the colour is assessed.

iii The quantity to be measured is the intensity of the colour produced after the biuret test has been carried out on the milk.

iv This could be measured by comparing the colours visually.

v If the hypothesis is correct, the purple colour formed in the cow's milk will be more intense than the colour in the goat's milk.

Exercise B3.03 Writing enzyme questions

Look for questions that are very clear, biologically correct and that have unambiguous answers.

Exercise B3.04 Lipase experiment

a fats (lipids)

b fatty acids and glycerol

c Fatty acids are produced, which are acids and therefore have pH below 7.

d See Table A3.03

Tube	1	2	3	4	5
Temp / °C	20	20	0	40	100
Milk added?	no	yes	yes	yes	yes
pH at: 0 min	7.0	7.0	7.0	7.0	7.0
2 min	7.0	6.8	7.0	6.7	7.0
4 min	7.0	6.7	7.0	6.5	7.0
6 min	7.0	6.6	7.0	6.3	7.0
8 min	7.0	6.6	6.9	6.2	7.0
10 min	7.0	6.5	6.9	6.2	7.0

Table A3.03

e There was no milk, so no fat, so no fatty acids were made.

f The high temperature denatured the lipase molecules, so there was no digestion of fats and no fatty acids were made.

g These tubes differed only in their temperature. Lipase acts more rapidly at 20 °C than at 0 °C because its molecules (and those of its substrate) are moving round faster and therefore collisions between enzyme and substrate molecules happen more frequently and with more energy. This means the rate of reaction is faster at 20 °C than at 0 °C.

h 40 °C is certainly the temperature at which the enzyme worked fastest in this experiment, but the optimum could actually be somewhere either side of this – either a bit below or anywhere between 40 °C and 100 °C.

i The experiment could be repeated, to obtain another set of results, to see if these matched the first ones. Alternatively (or as well), three tubes could be set up for each temperature, and a mean calculated. To find a more precise value of the optimum temperature, more temperatures need to be tested on either side of 40 °C – say, 35 °C, 45 °C, 50 °C and so on. Once these results have been found, the temperature range can be narrowed down even more to keep moving in closer and closer to the optimum temperature.

j Take equal volumes of cow's and goat's milk. Add equal volumes of lipase to both samples. Keep the tubes at 40 °C for five minutes.

Measure the pH every two minutes.

Repeat the experiment three times, and calculate the mean pH for cow's milk and mean pH for goat's milk at each time interval.

The milk in which the pH drops faster is the one that contained most fat.

Exercise B3.05 Finding the optimum pH for amylase

a pH

b 1 to 14 (a narrower range would be acceptable)

c Using buffer solutions. Tubes could be set up using buffers for pH 1, 2 and so on.

d The volume and concentration of starch solution used should be kept constant. Do this by making up one lot of starch solution, keeping it well mixed, and measuring volumes using a syringe or other calibrated instrument. The volume and concentration of amylase solution should also be kept constant – do this as for the starch solution. The temperatures of all solutions too need to be kept constant – use water baths.

e The time taken for the starch to disappear should be measured. Take samples from the mixtures of amylase and starch at timed intervals (e.g. every minute); place them on a tile and add iodine solution. Record the colour. The time at which the sample does not go black with iodine solution is the time to record.

f Measure equal volumes of starch solution into six tubes. Add equal volumes of different buffer solutions, for pH 1, 3, 5, 7, 9 and 11, to each tube. Stand the tubes in a water bath at a known temperature (e.g. 30 °C). Measure equal volumes of amylase solution, and add them to the starch mixtures. Use a clean glass rod to take samples from each tube (a different glass rod for each, wiped clean between samples) and place them on a tile. Add iodine solution and record the colour obtained.

g Look for columns or rows for the pH and the time taken for the brown colour to disappear. In this case, the values written in the table would be times in minutes. Students may also like to show the colour each time a sample was tested, in which case the results table should also have columns or rows with headings for the time intervals. The results written in the table would then be colours.

h The sketch graph should have an *x*-axis labelled 'pH', and a *y*-axis labelled 'Time taken for starch to disappear / minutes'. The line should begin high at the lowest pHs, drop down to pH 7.5 and then rise again.

Exercise B3.06 How enzymes work

a

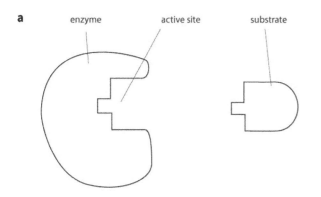

b

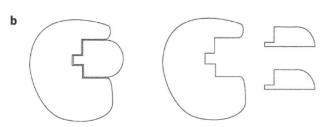

c i Each type of enzyme has an active site of a specific shape. It can only bind with a substrate whose shape is complementary to this.

ii The molecules of the enzyme and the substrate move faster at higher temperatures, so collide with each other more frequently.

iii Above its optimum temperature, an enzyme molecule loses its shape (becomes denatured), so the substrate cannot fit into its active site.

Chapter B4 Plant nutrition

Exercise B4.01 How a palisade cell obtains its requirements

- Light energy: from sunlight, which passes through **transparent epidermis** cells to reach the chlorophyll in the chloroplasts.
- Oxygen: by **diffusion** into the **air spaces** then out of a **stoma** into the air.
- Carbon dioxide: from the air, by **diffusion** through a **stoma** and then the air spaces in the spongy mesophyll.
- Water: from the soil, by **osmosis** into the **root hair** cells, then up through the stem in the **xylem** vessels, then by osmosis out of the xylem and into the palisade cell.
- Carbohydrates: stored as **starch** in the chloroplast, or changed to **sucrose** and transported away in the **phloem**.

Exercise B4.02 Sun and shade leaves

a The sequence of labels runs from **upper epidermis** at the top, then **palisade mesophyll**, then **spongy mesophyll**, and finally **lower epidermis** at the bottom of the diagram.

b Green spots should be put inside all the cells except those in the upper and lower epidermis; but guard cells should also contain green spots.

c See Table A4.01

Part of leaf	Sun leaf	Shade leaf
cuticle	relatively thick	relatively thin
palisade mesophyll	two layers	one layer
spongy mesophyll	more loosely packed; larger cells and more air spaces	quite tightly packed; small cells and small air spaces

Table A4.01

d The cuticle helps to prevent water loss from the leaf. The sun leaf will be hotter, so would tend to lose more water by evaporation, so the thicker cuticle helps to prevent this. The shade leaf has a thin cuticle so more of the limited amount of sunlight can get through it and reach the palisade cells.

e The sun leaf is exposed to much more sunlight, so having more palisade cells enables it to make more use of this light and photosynthesise more. There can be two layers of cells because at least some sunlight will penetrate through the top layer and reach those underneath. The shade leaf has much less light, so only very little would pass through the top layer of cells to reach a second layer, so there is no point in having a second layer of palisade cells.

Exercise B4.03 Analysing data about rates of photosynthesis

a Look for: 'Percentage concentration of carbon dioxide' on the x-axis, and 'Rate of photosynthesis / arbitrary units' on the y-axis; suitable scales; points plotted accurately, as crosses or encircled dots; best-fit lines drawn (though you could allow points joined with ruled lines); the two lines labelled 'low light intensity' and 'high light intensity'.

b 0.04%

c 53 arbitrary units

d 0.12% (Note that if students have drawn a best-fit line, their line may flatten a little before or after this value; if so, take the reading from their graph.)

e light intensity

f Carbon dioxide is often a limiting factor for photosynthesis, so adding more will make photosynthesis take place faster. This enables the plant to make more carbohydrates and grow faster, therefore producing higher yields.

g Around 0.08 to 0.10%. Above this, the increase in rate of photosynthesis is quite small (the graph is flattening off) so the extra yield is likely to be small.

Chapter B5 Animal nutrition

Exercise B5.01 Diet

a They all come from plants.

b Scrambled egg contains a large quantity of fat, which contains more energy per gram than any other nutrient.

c Spinach, because the total mass of the listed nutrients in 100 g of food is least, and therefore the remaining mass, which is mostly water, is greatest.

d Egg and spinach, as these have the highest concentrations of iron. Iron is needed to make haemoglobin. Anaemia is caused by a lack of haemoglobin.

Exercise B5.02 Functions of the digestive system

- Pepsin … in stomach
- Mastication … in mouth
- Gastric juice … in stomach
- Amylase … in mouth and in duodenum
- Pancreatic juice … in duodenum
- Lipase … in duodenum
- Bile salts … in duodenum
- Sodium hydrogencarbonate … in duodenum
- Saliva … in mouth.

Exercise B5.03 Tooth decay data analysis

a The incidence of tooth decay increases as standard of living decreases. Where the standard of living was highest, five-year-olds had a mean tooth decay score of 1.0 (that is, on average each child had one decayed tooth), but where standard of living was lowest they had a mean score of 4.0 (on average, each child had four decayed teeth).

b Perhaps children who have a low standard of living do not have as much calcium in their diet. Perhaps they do not clean their teeth or use fluoride toothpaste. Perhaps they eat more sweets or drink more carbonated drinks.

c This decreases the number of decayed teeth. We can see the difference between the results for town A and town B, where fluoride was added to the water. This roughly halved the number of decayed teeth in five-year-olds at any particular standard of living.

d Perhaps there is more fluoride in the naturally fluoridated water than was added to the water in town B. Perhaps the fluoride in town B has only been added recently, so the children didn't have fluoride in the water when they were younger.

Exercise B5.04 Vitamin D absorption

a It rose very rapidly over the first 12 hours, from 0 to just over 140 arbitrary units. After peaking at 12 hours, it fell less rapidly, reaching 60 a.u. at 8 hours. It then continued to fall but now very slowly, reaching 56 a.u. at 72 hours.

b small intestine / ileum

c glucose, amino acids, fatty acids, glycerol, water, any other vitamin, any mineral (e.g. calcium)

d It is long, so food is in contact with its walls for a long time. It is covered with villi, which increase its surface area. It is folded, which also increases surface area. The walls of the villi are thin, and there is a good blood supply, so it is easy for digested nutrients to diffuse through the walls and into the blood.

e Its molecules are already small enough to be absorbed.

f Vitamin D is made in the skin when sun shines onto it. If this had happened, we would not know how much of the vitamin D in the blood had come from this source, and how much from the vitamin D that was ingested.

Chapter B6 Transport in plants

Exercise B6.01 A transpiration experiment

a The results chart could look like Table A6.01:

Condition	Still air						Moving air				
Time / min	0	2	4	6	8	10	12	14	16	18	20
Distance / cm	0	2.8	6.1	10.0	12.9	16.2	21.8	27.9	31.1	39.5	44.9

Table A6.01

b Look for 'Time' on the *x*-axis and 'Distance' on the *y*-axis, both with units and sensible scales; points plotted accurately either as crosses or encircled dots; ruled straight best-fit lines drawn, with change in gradient sharp and clear at time 10 min.

c Still air: meniscus moved 16.2 to 0 = 16.2 cm in 10 minutes. So, mean rate was 1.62 cm per minute.

Moving air: meniscus moved 44.9 to 16.2 = 28.7 cm in 10 minutes. So, mean rate was 2.87 cm per minute.

d Yes. The mean rate per minute of movement of the meniscus is much higher in moving air than still air. This means that the shoot was taking up water faster in the moving air. The rate at which it takes up water is determined by the rate at which transpiration is taking place within the leaves.

e It is likely that the temperature was not controlled – it could have been warmer or colder in the moving air than in the still air. It is possible that light intensity was not controlled. The student was actually measuring the rate at which water was taken up, rather than the rate at which it was lost – but we can assume that they are very similar to each other, if not identical.

Chapter B7 Transport in mammals

Exercise B7.01 Double and single circulatory systems

a

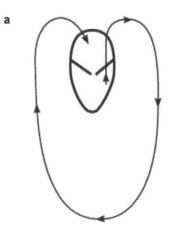

b human (*accept any mammal or bird*)

c fish (*accept any named fish*)

d In a double circulatory system, blood is returned to the heart after it has become oxygenated. The heart then pumps it at high pressure to the rest of the body. In a single circulatory system, the blood moves directly from the oxygenating organ (gills, lungs) to the rest of the body, at a relatively low pressure. A double system is therefore able to supply oxygen more quickly to respiring body cells, which allows metabolic rate to be faster.

Exercise B7.02 The heart in a fetus

a **O** in the left atrium.

b **OF** in the right atrium.

c It allows oxygenated blood to flow directly from the right atrium to the left atrium. This oxygenated blood then leaves the heart in the aorta, to deliver oxygen to respiring tissues all over the fetus's body.

d This prevents oxygenated blood in the left atrium mixing with deoxygenated blood in the right atrium. If they mixed, then there would be less oxygen in the blood in the aorta, so body tissues would not get as much oxygen delivered to them and would not be able to respire as fast. The tissues might run short of energy.

Exercise B7.03 Risk of heart attack

a She has a 13% (13 in 100) chance of having a heart attack in the next five years.

b She should stop smoking. This will reduce the risk from 13% to 7%. She cannot do anything about her diabetes. If she carries on smoking as she gets older, the risk of heart attack will rise to 22% when she reaches her 60s. If she stops smoking, it will only be 12%.

c Health records have been kept for large numbers of women over long periods of time. The records have been grouped into women in a particular age group, and into smokers and non-smokers, people with diabetes and people without. The percentage of people in each group having heart attacks has been worked out.

Exercise B7.04 Changes in the blood system at high altitude

a Look for some or all of the following ideas:
- the correct data being described – that is, the lighter grey bars
- reference to the overall trend – that is, pulse rate increases at high altitude

- reference to the fall during the period at high altitude
- reference to the initial fall and then rise when returning to low altitude
- some comparison of time scales – for example, the slow fall in pulse rate over the almost two years at high altitude, compared with the very rapid fall in just two weeks at low altitude
- reference to the slightly lower pulse rate at low altitude after having been at high altitude, compared with before travelling to high altitude
- at least two sets of figures quoted, stating both time and the value for pulse rate, including units.

b Look for some or all of the following ideas:
- the correct data being described – that is, the dark grey bars
- reference to the overall trend – that is, red blood cell concentration increases at high altitude but falls with time, then decreases again when at low altitude
- reference to the slightly lower concentration six weeks after having returned to low altitude, compared with before travelling to high altitude
- at least two sets of figures quoted, stating both time and the value for red blood cell concentration, including units.

c Oxygen transport.

d There is less oxygen available in the air at high altitude, so less diffuses into the blood. The person adapted to this by producing more red blood cells, to help to increase the amount of oxygen that could be absorbed into the blood and transported to body cells for respiration.

e A person who has trained at high altitude will have a faster pulse rate and more red blood cells. This will increase the rate at which oxygen can be supplied to muscles, making it possible for them to work faster because they can respire faster.

Chapter B8 Respiration and gas exchange

Exercise B8.01 Effect of temperature on the rate of respiration

Look for the following points being made somewhere in the plan:

- temperature varied, over a stated range (say, 0–50 °C)
- how the temperature is varied (e.g. placing in fridge, warm incubator, or standing in a water bath)
- important variables controlled – type and age of seeds, mass or number of seeds, length of time seeds are soaked before placing in a flask or other container, size and insulation of flask
- details of how the dependent variable (e.g. carbon dioxide concentration) will be measured
- outline results chart.

Exercise B8.02 Effect of animals and plants on the carbon dioxide concentration in water

a The results chart could look like Table A8.01:

Tube	A	B	C	D
Contents	animal only	plant only	animal and plant	no animal or plant
Colour of indicator at start	orange	orange	orange	orange
Colour of indicator at end	yellow	deep red	orange	orange

Table A8.01

Students might also want to include a row stating the conclusions that can be made.

b In tube A, the animal respired, giving out carbon dioxide.

In tube B, the plant photosynthesised (faster than it respired), taking in carbon dioxide.

In tube C, the carbon dioxide given out by the respiring animal was used by the photosynthesising plant, so there was no change in the carbon dioxide concentration in the water.

In tube D, neither photosynthesis nor respiration took place.

c Respiration would continue, but photosynthesis would not. The indicator would therefore go yellow in tubes A, B and C, and remain unchanged in D.

d During the day, aquatic plants take in carbon dioxide (and give out oxygen) which helps the animals in the tank. At night, the plants use oxygen and give out carbon dioxide, so this could mean less oxygen for animals for respiration, and a higher concentration of carbon dioxide in the water.

Exercise B8.03 Gas exchange surfaces in rats

a Look for:
- 'Age / days' on the x-axis
- 'Ratio of alveolar surface to body mass / cm² per gram' on y-axis
- both axes with suitable scales with equal intervals (not the intervals in the first column of the results chart)
- points accurately plotted as neat crosses or encircled dots
- two separate lines drawn
- a key or labelling to show which line is for females and which for males.

b The individual rats may have differed in size, so comparing the alveolar surface area for a small rat with that of a big rat would introduce another variable. The important feature is the ratio between surface area and mass or volume, as this gives information about how effectively the body cells (mass) can be provided with oxygen by the gas exchange surface.

c At 21 days, males have a higher ratio of surface area to body mass than females; the difference is 1.5 cm² per gram. However, from 33 days onwards, females always have a higher ratio than males. The greatest difference is at 95 days, when females have a ratio that is 4.0 cm² per gram higher than males.

d When pregnant, the female's alveolar surface has to supply the growing embryo, as well her own cells, with oxygen. She therefore needs a larger surface area in order to obtain this extra oxygen. This could explain why the female rats' ratio of alveolar surface area to body mass is higher than the males' ratio at 60 days (when pregnancy can first occur) and 95 days. (However, it does not explain why the ratio is actually at its highest at age 21 days, and then falls to age 45 days. This pattern is the same for both males and females, so perhaps this is related to the rate of growth of the rats at those stages in their development.)

Chapter B9 Co-ordination and homeostasis

Exercise B9.01 Caffeine and reaction time

Look for these points being made somewhere in the plan:
- caffeine intake varied (e.g. drinking coffee or cola and drinking water); some students may wish to use a range of caffeine concentrations
- important variables controlled: volume and concentration of caffeine in the liquid drunk; time between drinking and doing the reaction time test; time of day; age and sex of person; what the person has done just before the test is carried out; how many times the person has done a reaction time test before (in practice, it is impossible to control all of these variables)
- reaction time measured, using a stated method (e.g. using a test on the Internet, or catching a dropped ruler)
- repeats done (probably using different people, as any one person will improve as they do more tests, up to a limit)
- outline results chart drawn, and sketch graph showing predicted results if the hypothesis is correct.

Exercise B9.02 Accommodation in the eye

a

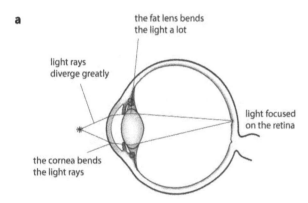

the fat lens bends the light a lot

light rays diverge greatly

light focused on the retina

the cornea bends the light rays

b The ciliary muscles contract, which narrows the diameter of the circle of muscles. This loosens the tension on the suspensory ligaments, which allows the lens to revert to its natural, rounded shape. The lens now refracts light rays more strongly, bringing the diverging rays from the nearby object to a focus on the retina.

c i A fast, automatic response to a stimulus.

  ii A blurred image on the retina.

d They are less able to focus on objects at different distances. They may be able to see clearly at a particular distance, but vision will be blurred at other distances.

Exercise B9.03 Auxin and tropism

a A response in which part of a plant grows away from the direction in which it is pulled by gravity.

b i Look for:
  - 'Time / minutes' on the *x*-axis
  - 'Percentage increase in length' on the *y*-axis
  - suitable scales on both axes
  - accurately plotted points using small crosses or encircled dots, neat best-fit lines
  - a key or labels to identify the two lines.

  ii There was more auxin on the lower surface than on the upper surface. This made the cells on the lower surface get longer than those on the upper surface, so the shoot curved upwards.

Exercise B9.04 Endotherms and ectotherms

a Endothermic animals: cat, rabbit, burrowing bettong

  Ectothermic animals: alligator, gopher snake, cyclodus lizard

b The cat, rabbit and burrowing bettong use respiration to provide heat to keep their bodies warm when the environmental temperature is below 37 °C. This requires fuel, which is in the form of carbohydrates, fats or proteins. The other three animals don't use food to produce heat energy, so they need much less.

c At 5 °C, the cat has a core body temperature of about 38 °C, so its metabolic reactions will be taking place quickly, and it will be active. The lizard has a body temperature of about 5 °C, so its reactions will be taking place slowly and it will be inactive.

d As they have a constant core temperature, cats are able to be active in winter and summer, at night and in the daytime. This means they can hunt in all seasons and at all times of day. Rabbits, too, can be active at all of these times, so they are able to flee from predators no matter what the external temperature.

Exercise B9.05 Diabetes

a When blood glucose levels rise higher than normal.

b The starch is digested by amylase (in saliva and pancreatic juice) to produce maltose. Maltose is digested by maltase to produce glucose. Glucose is absorbed into the blood capillaries in the villi in the small intestine.

c Person A. The blood glucose level rose higher after eating the starch, and stayed high for longer. In person B, insulin was secreted from the pancreas when the glucose rose above normal. This caused the liver to take some of the glucose out of the blood and change it into glycogen and store it. This did not happen in person A.

d If blood glucose concentration is too high, water is drawn out of the blood cells and body cells by osmosis. This means that metabolic reactions cannot take place normally in their cytoplasm. If blood glucose concentration is too low, cells do not get enough glucose to be able to carry out respiration, which is essential to supply them with energy for active transport and other processes.

Chapter B10 Reproduction in plants

Exercise B10.01 Pollination in forests of different shapes and sizes

a The most fruits per flower were produced in Area A, the set of patches of forest that were connected to each other by corridors. Here, there was an average of 0.5 fruits per flower. The least fruits per flower developed in the set of unconnected forest patches (Area B) and the set of smaller patches of forest came in between (Area C).

b Fruits will only develop after a flower has been pollinated. This is done by butterflies that prefer the edges of forests. So flowers near the edges of forests were more likely to produce fruits than ones deep inside. The small patches of forests had a larger edge (surface) to volume ratio than the large patches, and the patches joined by corridors had even more edges.

c There are many different suggestions students could put forward. For example, the researchers could make different patches of forest that were all identical in volume but had different lengths of edges, and compare the mean number of fruits per flower in each one.

d There are many possible answers to this question, and students are likely to put forward a range of ideas. In this particular case, it does appear that many small patches of forest are 'better' than a few big ones, but this is unusual

because these particular butterflies happen to need forest edges. There will be many more animals and plants that need large areas of deep forest to survive, and they will do better in large patches, preferably connected. Some animals need large territories in which to hunt. Some only need small areas, but there needs to be a large population to be sure they will not become extinct. Students may also refer to the importance of forests in the carbon cycle and in the production of oxygen.

Chapter B11 Reproduction in humans

Exercise B11.01 Gametes

a Black or blue labels: cell membrane, cytoplasm, nucleus.

b Red or other colour labels: look for about five labels altogether, each of which includes an explanation of the function of the feature. For example:

egg cell: haploid nucleus that will become a diploid nucleus when it fuses with the sperm nucleus

sperm cell: long tail to help it to swim to the egg.

Exercise B11.02 Gas exchange in the placenta and lungs

a The lungs are made up of millions of tiny alveoli. Although each of these is very small, there are so many of them that their total surface area is huge.

b **i** From the air spaces inside the alveoli, to the interior of the red blood cells in the capillaries.

ii There is a lower concentration of oxygen in the red blood cells than in the alveoli, because the blood has travelled past respiring cells that have taken oxygen from it and made it deoxygenated. There is a high concentration of air in the alveoli because fresh air is drawn in by breathing movements. Oxygen therefore moves by diffusion, down its diffusion gradient.

c The lungs have a surface area that is more than three times greater than the placenta, so more oxygen can diffuse across at any one moment in time.

The lungs have a thinner barrier than the placenta, so the diffusion distance is much smaller, and diffusion takes less time.

The rate of blood flow in the lungs is 10 times that in the placenta, so the oxygen is quickly taken away, maintaining a steeper diffusion gradient down which oxygen will diffuse more rapidly.

Chapter B12 Inheritance

Exercise B12.01 Fruit fly inheritance

a See Table A12.01

Genotype	Phenotype
NN	normal wings
Nn	normal wings
nn	vestigial wings

Table A12.01

B phenotypes of parents   normal wings   vestigial wings

genotypes of parents   Nn   nn

gametes   (N) and (n)   all   (n)

	gametes from vestigial-winged fly	
		(n)
gametes from normal-winged fly	(N)	**Nn** normal wings
	(n)	**nn** vestigial wings

c About half would have each phenotype, so about 41 with normal wings and 41 with vestigial wings.

Exercise B12.02 Black and chestnut horses

a i E

ii Ee

iii chestnut

b i **Ee** The foal must have had two **e** alleles, one from each of its parents. The mare was **ee**. The stallion was black, so he must have had one black allele and one chestnut allele.

ii phenotypes of parents   black   chestnut

genotypes of parents   **Ee**   **ee**

gametes   (E) and (e)   all (e)

	gametes from chestnut mare	
		(e)
gametes from black stallion	(E)	**Ee** black
	(e)	**ee** chestnut

So there was about a 1 in 2 chance that the foal would be chestnut.

iii Exactly the same: 1 in 2. Each time they have a foal, half of the stallion's sperm will be carrying an **E** allele and half carrying an **e** allele, so the chance of a sperm carrying an **e** allele fertilising the egg is 1 in 2.

Exercise B12.03 Pedigree

a Neither of the parents of the two people with PKU has PKU. If the allele was dominant, then at least one of the parents would have it and would therefore show the condition. This situation can only be explained if both parents are heterozygous, with one copy of the normal allele and one of the recessive PKU allele. Two of their children must have received the recessive allele from both parents.

b Both of person 4's copies of this gene are the recessive allele. It is virtually impossible for the same mutation to have occurred in both of them, as mutation is a random event.

c Person 1 could be either **QQ** or **Qq**. Person 2 could also be either **QQ** or **Qq**. Person 3 must be **Qq**, as they don't show the condition but do pass on a **q** allele to a child. Person 4 is **qq**.

Person 5 could be **QQ** or **Qq**, as both of her parents have the genotypes **Qq**.

d The only way person 5 could have a child with PKU is if she has the genotype **Qq** and her partner has this genotype as well. There is a good chance that she does not have the **q** allele (in other words that she is **QQ**) and it is likely that her partner will also be **QQ**. However, if she does have the genotype **Qq**, and if she marries someone from a family in which some members have PKU, then there is a risk that he could also be **Qq**, in which case there is a 1 in 4 risk of them having a child with PKU.

Chapter B13 Variation and selection

Exercise B13.01 Water hyacinth experiment

a 5 μm

b guard cell measures 12 mm in length = 12 000 μm

magnification = length in diagram ÷ real length

$\qquad$ = 12 000 μm ÷ 5 μm

$\qquad$ = × 2400

If the student has measured a different guard cell in the diagram, and arrived at a slightly different length value, the magnification value obtained will of course vary from that obtained here. Check that the method of calculation is correct.

c The leaves have many stomata on the upper surface. This is not usually found in land-living plants, where most stomata are on the lower surface to reduce the rate at which water vapour is lost through them – the lower surface is out of direct sunlight and therefore cooler, reducing the rate of evaporation and diffusion. The water hyacinth leaves are at the surface of the water, so they don't need to conserve water and having stomata on the upper surface allows them to absorb carbon dioxide easily from the air.

d The stomatal pores of the plants growing in polluted water are 1 μm smaller than those in clean water. The guard cells of the plants growing in polluted water are 2 μm shorter than those in clean water. The mean number of stomata on the upper surfaces of the leaves is the same in clean and polluted water. The mean number of stomata on the lower surfaces is a little higher in the plants growing in clean water than in those growing in polluted water.

Exercise B13.02 Big-horn sheep

a i nucleus

ii All of them. (All the body cells have a complete set of genes, but each type of cell only uses a particular number of them.)

b There has been selection against the sheep with the largest horns. Sheep with smaller horns are most likely to survive and reproduce. The alleles for smaller horns are therefore passed on to the next generations more often than the alleles for larger horns. Over time, more and more of the big-horn sheep population have small horns, and the mean horn length therefore decreases.

c i As the temperature rises, the sweat glands secrete more sweat onto the surface of the skin. The water in the sweat evaporates, taking heat with it and cooling the skin surface.

ii Vasoconstriction is the narrowing of the arterioles that supply blood to the skin capillaries. This reduces the amount of blood flowing close to the skin surface and therefore reduces the rate of heat loss from the blood to the air (by radiation). Instead, the blood is diverted to flow through deeper vessels, separated from the air by adipose tissue, which insulates the body and decreases heat loss.

Exercise B13.03 Goats on an island

a i A change in a gene or chromosome.

ii The long-hair allele, **a**, is recessive, so a goat needs two copies (one from each parent) in order to have long hair. Only goat **P** can pass on an allele for long hair, not the females, so none of its offspring could have long hair.

iii Some of the offspring from goat **P** would have inherited one copy of the **a** allele. If these bred with each other (or with goat **P**), then there would be a 1 in 4 chance of each offspring having the genotype **aa** and having long hair.

b i The long-haired goats did not lose as much heat from their well-insulated bodies, and so needed to generate less heat through respiration. They therefore needed less glucose (or other nutrients) to use as fuel in respiration.

ii The goats with long hair would have been at a selective advantage – they would be more likely to survive and breed than the short-haired goats. In each generation, there would therefore be more chance of the alleles for long hair being passed on than the alleles for short hair.

Exercise B13.04 Selective breeding for high milk yield

a i Value in 1990 = 11.0, value in 1965 = 7.2, so the change is an increase of 3.8 kg per cow.

ii Value in 1990 = 5.8, value in 1965 = 7.2, so the change is a decrease of 1.4 kg per cow.

b Only the cows that gave the highest milk yield would have been allowed to breed. They would be bred with bulls whose female family members also gave high milk yields. This would be done over several generations, each time only choosing the animals giving the highest milk yield to breed.

c   We can only guess – there is no evidence to tell us why the milk yield fell. In this group of cows, all the cows were equally likely to breed, so perhaps it is just chance that the mean milk yield fell over time. However, perhaps there is a disadvantage in having a high milk yield – for example, perhaps these cows were less healthy in other respects so they are actually less likely to have offspring.

d   i   The selected line were the cows with high milk yields. The large amounts of milk in their udders may have increased the incidence of inflammation, and the heavy weight of milk they have to carry around may have increased the degree of lameness.

   ii   They would need more food, to supply the materials needed to produce the extra milk.

Chapter B14 Organisms and their environment

Exercise B14.01 Energy transfer in a food chain

a   The position in a food chain at which an organisms feeds.

b   In sequence: producer, primary consumer, secondary consumer, tertiary consumer.

c   i $\dfrac{20}{20\,810} \times 100 = 0.1\%$

   ii   Much of it is lost as heat to the environment, through respiration. Some goes to the decomposer food chain.

d   i   There is not enough energy available at the higher trophic levels to support large populations.

   ii   By the time you reach a fifth or sixth link, there is not enough energy to support any organisms at all.

Exercise B14.02 Eutrophication

a   Plants need nitrogen-containing ions (such as ammonium or nitrate) to make proteins. They need proteins to build new cells, and therefore for growth. The soil in the field may be deficient in nitrogen-containing ions, which would limit the growth of the crop. The farmer therefore gets higher yields by adding these ions to the soil.

b   i   The population of algae rises rapidly just downstream of where the fertiliser flowed into the river. This is because algae can use the nutrients (nitrates and ammonium ions) in the fertiliser for growth. Further downstream, there are fewer nutrients because they have been used by algae upstream. The population size therefore decreases with the distance downstream.

   ii   Many of the algae die. The population of bacteria rises because they can feed on the increased quantity of dead algae. These bacteria use up the dissolved oxygen in the water in respiration. This decreases the quantity of oxygen. Fish need oxygen to respire, so either they die in the area where oxygen levels are low or they move away.

Exercise B14.03 Introduced species in New Zealand

a   They have wings, so they could fly across the oceans separating New Zealand from the nearest land.

b   Flight allows birds to escape predators. Predators are therefore a selection pressure which gives birds that can fly a greater chance of survival and reproduction. However, where there are no predators, there are fewer advantages in being able to fly, and there may be disadvantages. For example, birds that can fly use more energy than birds that cannot, they need to grow strong flight muscles, and they may need more food. Birds that do not have wings do not have these energy costs and may be better able to survive and reproduce, passing on their alleles for winglessness to their offspring. Over time, this process of natural selection will result in the whole population having no wings.

c   In all three areas, the number of seedlings in the areas where rats were trapped were greater than in the areas where they were not trapped. (Credit reference to comparative numbers of seedlings in any trapped and untrapped area.) Removing rats would therefore be expected to increase the population, as more seedlings would survive and grow into adult palms.